"We are living in an abundance of u........ advice, which is why we so desperately need voices who have done the work, plumbed the depths, and harvested true wisdom to guide us. I can think of no better way to describe the writings of Jen Pollock Michel. If you feel overwhelmed by your pace of life or your schedule feels like a bucking bronco, you will find more than simple, helpful steps in these pages, though they are many! You will also discover tender, theological riches."

Sharon Hodde Miller, author of *The Cost of Control*

"Here is a worthwhile meditation on how to steward the greatest resource that doesn't actually belong to us: time."

Justin Whitmel Earley, business lawyer and author of *The Common Rule* and *Habits of the Household*

"Once again, Jen Michel delivers. I was drawn by her honesty, storytelling, and practical wisdom. If you find yourself exhausted by the constant pressure to produce and long for a new way forward, her words will light the path."

Anjuli Paschall, author of *Stay* and *Awake*

"This book resonated deeply. Too many of us see time as a problem to be solved and a puzzle to be managed. But Jen Pollock Michel invites us to see time as a gift to be received and a mystery to be embraced. This book's wisdom is rich, immersive, beautifully written, and casually profound. Get yourself a copy and read it in an unrushed way."

Brett McCracken, senior editor at The Gospel Coalition and author of *The Wisdom Pyramid*

"Jen Michel uses words as her medium and paints gorgeous, soul-lifting art through her writing. A perfect blend of scholarly depth and lived experience, *In Good Time* offers hope, peace, and perspective for our hurried, anxious lives. Read slowly and savor this beautiful offering. I wholeheartedly recommend this book."

Vivian Mabuni, speaker, author of *Open Hands, Willing Heart*, and founder and podcast host of *Someday Is Here*

"Capacious in its heart and learning, *In Good Time* is just the sort of book we need to practice inhabiting time as clear-eyed, hopeful, and resilient disciples of Jesus."

Ashley Hales, PhD, author of *A Spacious Life* and *Finding Holy in the Suburbs*

"*In Good Time* is for all of us who imagine that the solution to our anxiety lies between the covers of the next great time management book. Jen Pollock Michel's wise and gentle reflections on learning new habits of being and receiving the lives we have been given are a balm for every soul weary from the relentless pursuit of productivity."

Amy Julia Becker, award-winning author of *To Be Made Well* and *White Picket Fences*

IN GOOD TIME

IN GOOD TIME

8 HABITS FOR REIMAGINING PRODUCTIVITY, RESISTING HURRY, AND PRACTICING PEACE

JEN POLLOCK MICHEL

BakerBooks

a division of Baker Publishing Group
Grand Rapids, Michigan

Published by Baker Books
a division of Baker Publishing Group
PO Box 6287, Grand Rapids, MI 49516-6287
www.bakerbooks.com

Printed in the United States of America

Library of Congress Cataloging-in-Publication Control Number: 2022014660
ISBN 978-1-5409-0054-8 (paperback)
ISBN 978-1-5409-0263-4 (casebound)

The author is represented by Alive Literary Agency, www.aliveliterary.com.

Some names and details have been changed to protect the privacy of the individuals involved.

Baker Publishing Group publications use paper produced from sustainable forestry practices and post-consumer waste whenever possible.

22 23 24 25 26 27 28   7 6 5 4 3 2 1

To my children:
Audrey, Nathan, Camille, Andrew, and Colin.
Thank you for your patience with me.
I love who you are and are becoming—
all in good time.

CONTENTS

However many be the days remaining to me,
I will do all things for the love of God.

Brother Lawrence

PART 1

ON
TIME
ANXIETY

In the Year
of Our Lord 2020

When the cloud of the pandemic grew dark, we were—of all places—at the beach. Toronto's airport had been crowded on the day of our departure. The COVID-19 virus still felt like a distant, foreign crisis.

The sky was cloudless after our arrival. Every morning, I woke early to watch the sun rise like a yolk in the sky. My husband, Ryan, on the other hand, was waylaid by a stomach bug. Most of the week he saw little more than the tiled bathroom floor.

We were taking our first beach vacation with four of our five kids, as our oldest was off to college: Nathan, a high school senior; Camille, a high school sophomore; Andrew and Colin, twin seventh graders. They scheduled their days around meals and multiple trips to the snack bar, filling up on fries before dinner. Every morning, water aerobics began promptly at 11:00 a.m., as the speakers blared "YMCA" and the pool filled with people.

Then without warning the utensils disappeared from the buffet lines, replaced by small bottles of hand sanitizer. Soon, staff were standing at every restaurant entrance and exit, pumping the antibacterial protection into guests' hands. On Thursday, one day after the WHO declared COVID's historic news, I spent an entire morning pleading by phone with Audrey, our oldest daughter, who was living in a dormitory on McGill's Montreal campus, to come home.

Initially, this was a crisis to last six weeks. Six weeks we would absent ourselves from the bustle of normal life. Six weeks we planned to stay home. But six weeks did not solve the crisis or leave it behind. By May, as graduations and summer camps canceled, as many colleges and universities planned for a virtual return in the fall, *normal* was a receding shore, growing ever more distant.

"We're living the Lord's time!" my friend in California said to me over the phone six months later. Like many women, she felt tugged between professional and domestic life—between managing her three children's virtual learning and her pressing work deadlines. The home renovation that had stalled in March was again underway, and she was managing that too. Pandemic time was a thousand years passing like a day, a day passing like a thousand years.

There has been no single experience of the COVID crisis, of course. In Toronto, where we endured the longest North American lockdown, some were shut in by deafening quiet in lonely downtown condos. Others lived a noisier year, small children constantly underfoot. For me, the crisis blew in like a storm and cut the engine of hurry; I welcomed, at least initially, the pause. But COVID did not turn out to be like a weather event. It was not a day for sledding and caramel popcorn, as when snow cancels school. No, this hardship brought a more foreboding change of climate.

Two years after the WHO's pronouncement on March 11, 2020, many companies had still not returned their employees to the office. Some, like my husband's company, have sold their headquarters and opted for a remote future, making the boundaries between home and work permanently porous. This is to say nothing of those who've lost lives and livelihoods in the last two years, those for whom the virus turned life over like a drawer and emptied it with hurricane force. For as much as we want to imagine the pandemic as something *past*, as something to forget, I fear it will long be with us, as trauma always is. Our bodies have a knack for remembering.

In the year of our Lord 2020, time wasn't just lived; it was *suffered*. And this is how Moses describes the experience of time in Psalm 90: "The years of our life are seventy, or even by reason of strength eighty; yet their span is but toil and trouble; they are soon gone, and we fly away."[1] Under virus conditions, life has felt suddenly brief, precarious.

I'm reminded of another large-scale catastrophe of this century—and the chapel talk Lisa Beamer gave at Wheaton College in 2016, fifteen years after the death of her husband, Todd, on September 11, 2001. Our family was on Wheaton's campus to celebrate my and Ryan's twentieth reunion, and the seven of us were at the back of the auditorium, sitting shoulder to shoulder in what might have been the very same row where two decades earlier

I'd recognized my freshman roommate from the picture she'd mailed me.

"Do you not know? Do you not hear?" Lisa read aloud from Isaiah 40. "It is he who sits above the circle of the earth, and its inhabitants are like grasshoppers." For her text that morning, she had chosen a strange passage from the prophet that begins with pleas for comfort, then slips into darker musings about mortality. I could picture that swarm of humanity as she read aloud, the throb and thrum of them scurrying after their important, microscopic business. Her voice caught.

"Scarcely are they planted, scarcely sown, scarcely has their stem taken root in the earth, when he blows on them, and they wither, and the tempest carries them off like stubble."[2] I remembered the day when Manhattan's Towers of Babel fell, the city disappearing in plumes of smoke, the sky raining the ticker tape of global commerce. I remember when United Flight 93 ran aground somewhere in the middle of Pennsylvania.

How brief it is, *time*. How very, very small our stature.

Playing Busy like a Fiddle

As early as April 2020, a debate raged about the responsibilities of those of us turned safely inside during this global storm. For those time privileged enough to find their calendars suddenly cleared, what should we do with all this newfound *time*? Should we perfect our baking skills? Learn another language? Launch a business? Organize the pantry and the photo albums? The *New York Times* regularly featured exactly these sorts of ideas, and I did feel better when, on a spring Saturday, we hung garage shelving to organize bikes, sports equipment, and snow shovels.

But in her article for *Wired*, writer Laurie Penny took issue with those "lucky enough to be able to shelter in place," who were "using that time to launch podcasts and personal projects and life-hack [their] way to some cargo-cult pastiche of normality."[3] In her essay, Penny defiantly opposed the idea that we were most optimized when we were most productive. "Productivity," she argued, "is not a synonym for health, or for safety, or for sanity."

"How shall we stay productive," Penny asked, "when the world is going to hell?"

It was a question to which I felt particularly attuned. *Busy* has long been the most recognizable version of me.

In college, I snagged a copy of *Disciplines of the Beautiful Woman* from my freshman roommate's bookshelf. The book was a study in spiritual practices like prayer, Bible study, and regular church attendance. It was also a collection of productivity hacks: keeping a calendar, organizing a desk, managing a filing system, and when the occasion called for it, finding the perfect dress on the sale rack in record time. "Here is a list of things you can do when you're tempted to dawdle—or watch TV indiscriminately," the book suggested.[4]

After college graduation, I was hired to teach French and English at a high school on Chicago's North Shore. Within months of my hiring, my department chair persuaded me to apply for graduate school. "It's never going to get any easier," he said, wearily nodding at the picture of his two young children atop his desk. For the next several years, I rarely found time to plan ahead. Once, on the way to my sister-in-law's bridal shower, where guests were expected to wear white, I zipped into the parking lot of a suburban Chicago mall and gave myself exactly twenty minutes in Marshall Field's to find an outfit. I found a close parking spot and the perfect dress hanging near the door. *Godspeed*, I told myself.

Even when I quit my teaching job and became an at-home mother, I worked to make my domestic life as busy as my professional one. When our twin boys arrived in 2008, there was no need to go looking for busy. Getting out of the house with five children ages seven and younger became a military exercise. There were strings of days I didn't remember to brush my teeth. Even my long-held habit of immersive Bible reading gave way to months of meditating on one simple psalm, Psalm 145, which I copied on a couple of index cards and tucked into the pocket of my nursing chair. I slept when the babies slept, figuring that God understood how busy—and very, very tired—I was.

Both Ryan and I have played busy like a fiddle. "Every big career needs a wife," Stephen Marche's father told him when his wife, Sarah Fulford, took the job as (youngest) editor-in-chief for *Toronto Life*.[5] I've been that wife—to that kind of career. Ryan finished his professional actuarial designation at thirty, then applied to MBA programs, moving our family from Ohio to accept an offer from the University of Chicago. (I gave birth three weeks later.) He attended classes part-time while continuing to climb the corporate ladder, and I was left alone many nights for dinner and baths and bedtime.

"How do you do it?" I have often been asked. When the kids were younger, I did "it" by strapping the youngest in the Costco cart and barking reminders to the older ones, walking alongside, to hold tight.

There has not been a season of life I've left to dawdling: not when I was a high school senior, leaving school several times a week to practice my piano for my senior recital; and not in the year of our Lord 2020, when a global health crisis shut the world down. Time (for me at least) has acted like a lash held in the hands of some imperious master. This penchant for productivity is part personality, to be sure—but it is also part formation. I'm an American Protestant, after all, and I understand that God wants us to get things done.

"We must remember," Jeremy Taylor writes in his sixteenth-century *The Rule and Exercises of Holy Living*,

> that we have a great work to do, many enemies to conquer, many evils to prevent, much danger to run through, many difficulties to be master'd, many necessities to serve, and much good to do, many children to provide for, or many friends to support, or many poor to relieve, or many diseases to cure, besides the needs of nature, and of relation, our private and our publick cares, and duties of the world.[6]

Holiness can read like a long, exhausting list.

But whatever our religious persuasion, today busyness is pushed upon all of us: as expectation, as duty. It's life's de facto characteristic. The days run swift and swollen like a river after rain, and time anxiety is one of humanity's most chronic pains.

How are you?

Busy.

According to Jesus, however, we are not the first humans worried by time. Before smartphones and time management apps, before digital calendars and even analog clocks, people have been plagued by time anxiety. In the Sermon on the Mount, Jesus addressed those first-century worriers with a host of practical advice. He wanted people to make peace by confronting and forgiving hurt. He gave commands for keeping promises and keeping marriages together. He forbade lust and the public performance of righteousness. He taught people to pray and to resist greed. This was not spiritual advice at its most ethereal nor faith at its most abstract. Jesus wasn't just teaching the *principles* of the kingdom of God but also its *practices.* Its habits, in other words.

Toward the end of that sermon, Jesus spoke to people on the hillside about time. Like us, these men and women found the days woefully short. "Which of you by being anxious can add a single hour to his span of life?" Jesus asked them.[7] His question can hardly be more resonant today. In fact, it's a question that's propped up an entire industry selling us on the moral imperative of time management. But Jesus did not sermonize about productivity and efficiency, about hustle and hurry.[8] Jesus did not thunder "Do more!" and "Run faster!" Rather, he reassured these ancient, anxious people of God's constancy and care.

If God remembered to feed the birds and clothe the flowers, what would he ever forget?

A Pandemic Disclosing

In the early months of 2020, time wound down like a neglected grandfather clock. At 8:00 a.m., I wasn't hurrying my children out the door for school. At 4:00 p.m., I wasn't embroiled in the afternoon rush to retrieve them. There was no need to organize the soccer car pool or drive my daughter to her weekly horseback riding lesson. Every speaking engagement was canceled. Saturdays contracted: no games, no gatherings, no errands. Sunday mornings trended simpler: homemade waffles and the 10:30 a.m. church service viewed from the basement.

Because I had more time, I resolved initially to give myself to productivity. I made recognizably ambitious lists: to read Montaigne, to make challah, to teach my children to properly clean a bathroom. I sent writing prompts to my mother and mother-in-law, imagining the memoir project I'd help them complete: "Tell a story about your parents, which captures how you remember them from childhood." I promised a start on this very book you're reading to my agent. "May—at the latest," I assured. And because someone convinced me I had an important historical duty, I began keeping a pandemic journal for posterity's sake. "Call it your Coronavirus diary, your plague journal, whatever. It's important. Later, you will want a record."[9] In the fall, I started to index its hundreds of pages.

Compared to so many—the sick, the dying, the incarcerated, even the young family next door—I had very little reason for complaint. We had a backyard and blooming rhododendrons. We were employed and healthy. My children were self-sufficiently managing their remote learning, and I was making bread, even writing poems about those loaves: *In rising light, I stumble to the kitchen and stand in service of the yeast: I'll make the bread again that God won't eat.*

By contrast, I watched the father next door flicking rubber hockey pucks into the net, day after day, with his young son, Tommy. I watched them add play equipment to their backyard: a trampoline, monkey bars, a slip 'n' slide, and eventually a small above-ground pool. Without siblings, without a regular school routine, Tommy had idle hours his parents were conscripted to fill.

What was my problem, then? Why, for all my privilege, for all my efforts at productivity, was time still a throbbing fist in my chest?

Here was the dislocation of the year of our Lord 2020—or better, its *disclosing*. I had time, but it solved little. The days slowed, and I was catching up to myself—yet I still couldn't seem to live the unhurried, unworried time of the Lord.

YOLO

My iPhone buzzes at 5 a.m., and the week starts with a lurch. It's Monday, and it's dark. I silence my alarm and lie a little longer in bed, thinking of the letter my son Nathan wrote to himself six years ago, when he was in the seventh grade. We found it yesterday, tucked in his diploma. After the disappointments and delays of the year of our Lord 2020, we have finally celebrated Nathan's graduation virtually, a whole year late.

The letter reads, "Another thing I'd like to talk about is Jesus. He has been the Lord of my life even though at times I have struggled to keep him close. I hope you still love him today. Never stop praising, confessing, or obeying." Those words arrive from years ago, and I wonder about their hold on my doubting Thomas son. That profession of childhood faith? Today, it's a thing of the past, and I worry after it.

I pad downstairs to make coffee, then settle myself, like a sentry, in a chair in my living room. "I wait for the LORD, my soul waits, and in his word I hope; my soul waits for the Lord more than watchmen for the morning, more than watchmen for the morning."[1] Through the front window,

I see an older man shuffle by, zipped in a gray tracksuit. In my journal, I scribble answers to a few examen questions, then copy Proverbs 3:1–8 as a text to pray over my daughter, who has just left for summer camp in the States. For her, too, I hang by threads of faith. How can she be made to know this wisdom that is better than jewels, that all she might desire cannot compare with it?

Soon the oven timer buzzes. Not quite a monastery bell and not quite an hour, but it signals the end to my prayer and my day's assigned Bible reading. I haven't finished—no, I'm simply hurried along. Upstairs, I lace up my running shoes, then transfer yesterday's wash to the dryer. I run down two flights to the basement, then open my exercise app.

Thirty minutes later, sweaty, I rush to find my computer and my prayer book. By the time I open our small group prayer meeting at 7:00 a.m. via Zoom, Caroline is waiting. Kent and Johnny join soon after. David texts that he and Hailey will be missing, and I assume that my husband, somewhere in the house, has forgotten.

"Invitation," I read. "You, Lord, are my lamp; the Lord turns my darkness into light." The top of the page tells me that it is "Ordinary Time." The daily readings are taken from Psalm 142 and Ephesians 2.

It is a Monday: a day for beginning and beginning again.

As I read the first ten verses of Ephesians 2 aloud, I notice in Paul's letter all that God is doing *in time*: "As for you, you were dead in your transgressions and sins."[2] Paul is describing something past, something that might have once seemed unalterable: death. I think of fossils hardening, of layers upon layers of geometric rock. Time, writ indelible. *We were dead.* I think of Mr. W. J. Turner, described by Dr. Dugdale in the first chapter of her book *The Lost Art of Dying*. A frail and elderly man dying of cancer, Mr. Turner coded three times and was resuscitated twice. The last time, "after twenty minutes of CPR, the code team leader performed the ritual that seals the fate of the recently deceased: he called off the code. This time, there would be no raising the dead."[3]

It would seem that death is time irretrievable—a river not to be reversed. But as I read, I can't help but see the past is never fixed with God. With God, what *was* is always subject to change. The dead are resuscitated. *Raised.* With God, what *was* does not determine what *will be.* "But . . . God, who is rich in mercy, made us alive with Christ even when we were dead in transgressions."[4]

This next verse sets me to thinking of God's mercy, this wide and generous berth granted to sinners. Mercy is God acting in time with long-suffering, with patience. Mercy represents God's ability to wait. I recall the refrain from the book of Hebrews: "Today, if you hear his voice, do not harden your hearts."[5] It sets me to wondering, Does God's mercy make every day a *today?*

Reading further still, I see purpose and forethought in the scheme of God's saving work. Before we left off all our God-forsaking ways, while we were stubbornly yet sinners, we were "created in Christ Jesus to do good works, which God prepared in advance for us to do."[6] Maybe time anxiety could be swallowed up here, in God's promise to make poetry of our lives.

Which of you, by being anxious, can add a single hour to the stature of your lives?

We have been raised with Christ and "seated . . . with him in the heavenly realms," Paul writes.[7] I think of myself there and then, in the world beyond the veil—and here and now, in this chair, God holding time in his hands as capably as he holds the whole world. I think about how long redemption has been set in motion, how we are simply carried along, today, in the steady current of his divine power and love. "Thus am I, a feather on the breath of God."[8] I think of how little fretting must be required for these good works he's planned for us, the works to which he's already affixed our names. Like the curbside order we picked up Saturday on the way to the birthday party: someone wheeled it to the car, and Ryan lifted it into the trunk.

For one brief, faith-filled moment, I manage to remember there is always enough time to do what God has planned. I consider the freedom, the careless joy of living and moving and having my being in God. I grasp a glimpse of the unpanicked life, of resting in the knowledge of days held in God's palm.

Then we end the call, and soon enough I am bullying my way into another Monday morning. I run upstairs to take the sheets from the dryer and make my daughter's bed; she is now halfway to her camp in Wisconsin. I plan to read a hundred pages of a book, write an annotation for graduate school, and finish an essay.

By 2:00 p.m., I haven't checked a single thing off my list.

Problem-Solving Time

For thirty years, I've been a reader of time management books. As someone else has put it, this is to say I have indulged the "pleasure entertained in the fantasy that time can be managed."[9] I began reading these books in college and continued when my kids were small. Though I was not managing a big corporate career like my husband, when he brought home Katharine Graham's autobiography from a graduate school class, I planned for things beyond diapers and laundry. I knew time was instrument to ambition.

My swelling time anxieties in 2020 set me on a jag of reading (and rereading) productivity books. It was my friend Adam who first introduced me to David Allen's classic, *Getting Things Done,* in our shared season of raising young children. Now I revisited Allen's book—updated, since I'd first read it, to accommodate our new digital landscape.

Allen's argument is simple: we are anxious about time because we don't have fail-safe systems. Until we can reliably capture and retrieve the many bits of information we feel responsible for, we can't be rid of the nagging fear something has been forgotten. Until we make comprehensive lists, then develop routines for reviewing those lists and planning for the week, month, and year ahead, we will be constantly subject to anxiety. In Allen's view, time anxiety can be solved by time competency. For every new time worry, there is a new time technique.

I also reread Greg McKeown's *Essentialism,* a book assigned to staff members of a church where I served years ago. Unlike Allen, McKeown is more philosophical than practical in his approach to managing time. He doesn't offer advice for culling old files and clearing off our desks. Instead, McKeown insists that before we organize our calendars, we must articulate our priorities.

Time anxiety, according to McKeown, is solved by living courageously according to our values. There isn't enough time for everything, but there is time for what really matters in our personal and professional lives. McKeown's question is, Will we discipline ourselves to pursue that purposeful *less*?

After Allen and McKeown, I dug deeper into the work of Laura Vanderkam. Unlike many of the predominantly male time management experts, whose advice often assumes, if not a partner, then a very capable staff, Vanderkam is, like me, a wife and mother of five. Her research explores how professional women get it "all" done.

In *I Know How She Does It*, Vanderkam reveals findings from the time diaries of women earning more than $100,000/year, and her conclusions ring with optimism. There's more time than we think! With 168 hours in a week, 8,760 hours in a year, and on average, 700,000 hours in a lifetime, we don't need more time, we just need more creativity. Vanderkam advises women to lower expectations for housework, hire help as needed, quantify the hours, and appreciate, based on the data, how much time you really spend with your kids. According to her own time diary, the dual commitment to domestic and professional ambition might find you in an Amtrak bathroom pumping breastmilk at odd hours of the day or night.[10]

In search of time equilibrium, I also revisited Matt Perman's *What's Best Next*. "More important than efficiency is effectiveness—getting the right things done," he writes. A Christian, Perman insists we need more than good time management strategies; we need virtue. This isn't to dispense with the practicalities of time management, in Perman's view: "This downplaying of the practical is not only discouraging but actually an (unwitting) failure of *love*."[11]

In the book, Perman offers his own time map for a typical week, suggesting ways that readers might envision prioritizing family, work, leisure, and spiritual formation. Noting that four days a week, Perman dedicated the hour between 5:00 and 6:00 p.m. for "exercise," I once published a grouchy review of Perman's work: "I'd like to see his wife's time map."[12]

In all these books, I could see time had one inflexible demand, one irreducible urgency. *Productivity*. I needed to find more efficient ways to get things done and account—materially—for the efforts of a day.

It was only later that I came to understand I was gaining no new insights from any of these books. The time management industry, according to Melissa Gregg, author of *Counterproductive*, was a one-trick pony: "ranked and refined To Do lists; daily affirmations; time logs; single handling; delegation; embracing seclusion."[13] As the Teacher of Ecclesiastes might have said it, a man as much preoccupied as I with questions of time, there was little new under the time management sun.

In fact, I might as well have been reading Catharine Beecher's *The American Woman's Home*, cowritten with her sister, Harriet Beecher Stowe, in 1869. In Section XXVII, "Habits of System and Order," she tells women they must get up early or find some quiet pocket of the day to

> seek strength and wisdom from the only true Source. At this time, let her take a pen, and make a list of all the things

which she considers duties. Then, let calculation be made, whether there be time enough, in the day or the week, for all these duties. If there be not, let the least important be stricken from the list, as not being duties and therefore to be omitted.[14]

Above all else, a woman could not fail "the systematic employment of time."[15]

Making It Count

The systematic employment of time has a long history—and immersing oneself in ideas for practically organizing the day serves as the kind of faux-productivity that Walter Chen and Rodrigo Guzman identified after founding iDoneThis, a productivity tool that tracked what users accomplished in a day. Initially, users were content to simply quantify what they did with their hours. Soon, however, they began demanding more features. They wanted to plan future projects; they wanted to manage their to-do lists.

Chen and Guzman met these user demands but were to quickly learn that "fully 41 percent of to-do items on iDoneThis were never done." It seemed people loved to write to-do lists but were notoriously uncommitted to those lists. Those lists, in fact, came to remind them of their *failures* in and with time. They became "lists of shame."[16]

But if to-do lists are this demonstrably unhelpful, why are productivity apps such big business? Why did Americans download them 7.1 billion times in 2020?

The reason has more to do with existential consolation, according to Clive Thompson in an article for *Wired*:

"To-do lists are, in the American imagination, a curiously moral type of software. . . . With to-do apps, we are attempting nothing less than to craft a superior version of ourselves. Perhaps it shouldn't be a surprise that when we fail, the moods run so black."[17] In other words, our to-do lists catalog more than ambition. They inscribe the meaning we need to eke out of our lives. They give us the assurance that if we keep the hours productively, our lives will achieve some lasting value, something that the tides of time can't carry away.

To say it most forcefully, our to-do lists hedge against mortality. "Every single time you write down a task for yourself," writes Thompson, "you are deciding how to spend a few crucial moments of the most nonrenewable resource you possess: your life. Every to-do list is, ultimately, about death."[18]

Life Hack

On a mild August morning in 2021, Ryan and I walked our three boys and their cousins to a park in Chicago's Ukrainian Village. After a year and a half of closed borders and separation from our extended families, we were taking a grand tour through the American Midwest to celebrate our reunion.

First we visited my mother and her ailing husband of twenty-seven years in central Ohio. My stepfather is suffering the slow ravages of Parkinson's disease, and he mostly uses a wheelchair now. Our daily activities were planned around his morning and afternoon naps, limited to terrain in which we could comfortably navigate pushing him. On the second leg of the trip, we visited Ryan's family, renting a house west of the Chicago River where his mother, his brother, his sister, and their families could all gather.

In a small patch of summer shade in a municipal park, Ryan and I sipped iced coffee while the five boys played basketball. We were discussing a major life decision—a disruption of pandemic proportions. We considered alternatives, weighed options, wondered aloud about God's leading.

Like most decisions, the alternatives circled around questions of time: of ultimate things, of final things. What mattered? What mattered now? What couldn't be put off? What made sense of God's revealed will in Scripture? The decision begged the prayer of Moses in Psalm 90:12: "Teach us to number our days that we may gain a heart of wisdom."

That's when we saw the billboard.

Off the Kennedy expressway, a block beyond the park, was a billboard that practically shouted an answer to the questions we sat asking each other. Let's just say that, had we been considering a move to Brazil, the billboard would have read, "Learn Portuguese fast!" Had we been wondering whether to sell the house and travel the country in an RV, the billboard would have boasted a map and a rebate code.

I elbowed Ryan. "Look at that!"

God might very well write his will on billboards, and I could have been made to believe in the possibility on that summer day in 2021, when an emphatic answer to our questions about moving back to the States—to be closer to family—glared back at us in towering letters of black and white: "Move to Ohio." I could assume Ryan and I were being shepherded into decisiveness, that we were being spared complications and mistakes. After all, didn't I believe in bushes that burned, in fleeces so wet they had to be wrung dry? Didn't I insist a star guided an ancient caravan of men across months and thousands of miles, bringing them finally to the place where Jesus lay swaddled in his mother's arms?

God can certainly use billboards, should they be required.

But I had darker suspicions—reasons to mistrust my own enthusiasms. Maybe my belief in billboards had less to do with my confidence in God and my trust in his shepherding love. Maybe it had more to do with the disordered ways I inhabit time and prize, above all else, "optimization." To think how much more *efficient* it would be if God would micromanage our paths, calling out directions in the recognizable voice of Siri.

If only God had as much preoccupation for the "wasting" of time as we do.

This isn't God's way, of course. He is not the huffing father at the wheel of the car, parked in front of the school and wondering what's keeping his kids so long after practice. In the Bible, God is not caught tapping his foot or checking his watch, bemoaning how long it takes his people to move. Sure, there is that moment in the book of Jonah when God hurls howling winds and a hungry whale to steer the prophet back on course, but generally, God has a reputation for patience. "I am *slow* to anger," God announced to Israel. I have no reason for panic.

Living into Wisdom

If God's only interest was to save time, he would not dither with the plodding business of forming wisdom in his people. Wisdom, as our moral capacity for deciding, is not something to be hurried. God could very well lead us forcibly, like a parent threading a small child by the hand through a thicket of people at an amusement park. Or he could train our feet to travel his paths.

Wisdom, in other words, is not the efficient business of hacking life. It is not the product of searching Google and scrolling social media. Nor is it a matter of applying tips and tricks to the thorny problems of being human. No, wisdom has nothing to do with technique and its proposed efficiencies. That's why it rarely factors into time management advice, which is largely preoccupied with questions of *how* rather than *why*. Instead, wisdom is fruit borne from the fear of the Lord.[1] Wisdom is formed incrementally by a long and slow obedience to God. In fact, wisdom, as a product of character, cannot be had all at once. "It takes time," writes Ellen Davis, "for the tree of human experience to bear the fruit of wisdom."[2]

To read billboards, you don't need wisdom. At my age, you simply need glasses.

If God only cares for our punctual arrival at the place of his choosing, he could electrify our path like an airport runway. But efficiency doesn't seem to be God's project. No, God longs to see wisdom formed in his people: "Be not like a horse or a mule, without understanding, which must be curbed with bit and bridle, or it will not stay near you."[3] He longs to see us submit to his instruction, his teaching, his counsel—these levers of wisdom. He longs to form in human beings greater and greater capacity for trust.

A donkey can follow the lights of a blinking billboard. But wisdom, as Derek Kidner writes, "is for disciples only."[4]

My interest in the Wisdom Literature of the Bible (primarily the books of Job, Proverbs, and Ecclesiastes) was rekindled recently as I prepared to speak on the topic of womanhood at my church. My text was Proverbs 31:10–31, a familiar passage that has plagued many Christian women. Proverbs 31 has been read like an impossible to-do list for women trying to do it "all."

If there is a woman who knows how to muscle time from a day, we find her in Proverbs 31.

This *eshet hayil*,[5] or woman of valor, is industrious and resourceful, tireless and early rising. She sews. She invests in real estate. She works a side hustle. Apparently, this valorous woman is also endlessly cheerful. She is not given to my own weary and angry tirades that start with, "I don't see Cinderella working here!" She doesn't grouse about crumbs on the counter, toilet lids yawning open, lidless cups of coffee that spill in the car on the way to school. No, her children rise up and call her blessed.

"You aren't meant to imitate this woman exactly," I tell the conference attendees through my Zoom camera. "This passage acts like a parable, illustrating in the landscape of everyday life what it would look like to live by the principles of wisdom laid out in the rest of the book."

This passage is not a Butterick sewing pattern, I reassure. To achieve the Proverbs 31 standard, if it were to exist, either as a model for womanhood or a template for time management, a woman would have to be wealthy enough to dress herself in fine linen and purple and to afford investment properties. And she would need more than socioeconomic privilege. She would also have to be able-bodied. She could not suffer from chronic illness and keep the kind of grueling schedule this woman keeps, rising while it's still night and ensuring that her lamp never goes out.

Instead, Proverbs 31:10–31 is a twenty-two-line acrostic poem, traditionally memorized by Jewish husbands to sing over their wives during the Shabbat meal. Notably, the only command given in the passage, in verse 31, is addressed to the husband of this noble, competent, excellent, God-fearing woman: "Give her of the fruit of her hands, and let her works praise her in the gates."

Wisdom is far more concerned with ethical practice than type-A respectability. According to Old Testament scholar Derek Kidner, wisdom is about a human's "management of affairs, his sensitivity to people, his character and his morals; above all . . . his relation to God."[6] Wisdom, then, cannot be measured by the stopwatch, as productivity can be measured. A stopwatch can count the seconds, but it cannot measure virtue and the beauty of holy living.

Kidner points out that Wisdom Literature in the Bible requires us to step into a participatory role. It assumes the exercise of human agency and asks us, given the fear of the Lord, to decide. It does not speak in the mode of the Law: *thou shall*. Neither does it speak in the mode of the Prophets: *thus sayeth the Lord*. Rather, Wisdom Literature engages the reader and "draws [them] into answering and asking, into working things out painfully."[7] Wisdom is the capacity Ryan and I were left to exercise that day in the summer shade while we sipped iced coffee. We needed wisdom when none of the available options (except the very obvious billboard) blinked glaring lights of call or caution.

Responsibility—in this life—cannot be avoided.

"'The fear of the LORD is the beginning,' or first principle, 'of wisdom,'" writes Kidner. "In one form or another, this truth meets us in all the wisdom books."[8]

Time Privilege

For Christmas, our son Nathan asked for and received—from his apprehensive grandmother—a copy of *The Meditations* by Marcus Aurelius, a second-century Roman emperor. Although it's not the book most nineteen-year-old boys are likely reading, Nathan is a philosophy major—in love with (*philo*) this business of wisdom (*sophos*). Late one Friday night, he reads some passages to me over FaceTime, and we talk about the disappearance of wisdom traditions today, generations no longer passing along time-tested truths about living and dying.

It strikes me that time management books figure as contemporary wisdom literature. If the task of ancient wisdom literature was to instruct readers "in the art of living well,"[9] the same impulse beats at the center of today's time management books. As Oliver Burkeman points out in his book *Four Thousand Weeks: Time Management for Mortals*, we don't simply try managing our time to ply more minutes from the day. We want more *meaning*.[10]

We're all afraid of missing it. The good life.

There are, of course, glaring differences between the *technique* of time management and the long-haul learning of biblical wisdom. In many ways, time management offers a facsimile of real wisdom. The Wisdom Literature of the Bible imagines the good life as a life submitted and surrendered to God; the humanist wisdom of time management, by contrast, is preoccupied with different questions entirely. It relies on no moral or philosophical framework. Productivity is a measure, not of good, but of output. As Melissa Gregg puts it, time management generates a "self-affirming logic for action."[11] Its wisdom is one of means, rather than ends.

Productivity "wisdom" has other problems too. Unlike biblical wisdom, which assumes diversity and difference, time management relies on an ethic that excludes. I can't imagine my friend Constance having much real interest in modern time management conversations, not as an immigrant and single mother of three. Although there was the day I arrived at her apartment and noticed a portable foot spa sitting in a box by the kitchen doorway—"I got it free on Facebook!"—she does not enjoy many superfluous conveniences.

When my friend first arrived in Canada and faced a slew of both medical and immigration appointments, an early investment was a calendar, something she'd never owned before where she lived previously. Her new North American life filled those small rows of squares. Five years after her "landing," as it's called in Canada, my friend remains extraordinarily busy—but I never hear her ask, "How do I manage my time?" She simply stays up past midnight to finish her homework for the vocational certification she's currently pursuing. "I need a job," she tells me constantly. I tell her she has many.

The historically recent time management conversation is a privileged one. In the early twentieth century, Frank and Lillian Gilbreth brought Frederick Winslow Taylor's principles of scientific management into the home, where they raised their twelve children. The Gilbreths looked to apply the standards of efficiency and productivity to the home, famously adopting Gantt charts to run their busy household.

But it wasn't the Gilbreths' time savvy alone that allowed them to manage their busy professional and domestic lives. Both Frank and Lillian employed full-time secretaries for their writing and had as many as seven full-time assistants as well as a live-in grandmother to assist with the child-rearing. They had time—because they also had money to afford help.[12]

Wealth is one important measure of time privilege, but it isn't the only one. When Sara Hendren gave birth to Graham in 2006, she and her husband learned Graham had Down syndrome. As Graham grew, Hendren came to recognize the temporal bias of the child development conversation: a child was always measured against a normative timeline. He was either *behind* or *advanced*. But because Graham developed at his own pace, he seemed inevitably mismatched to the timekeeping of the clock-watching world.

Hendren began to understand what disability scholars have come to call "crip time," which "is flexible shorthand in disability culture, used to indicate a range of uneasy relationships to the pace of contemporary industrialized life, with its relentless and clock-driven reorganization of hours and days."[13] Crip time requires that people measure time differently and account for the different ways different people move through the world. Crip time is not the time *tasks* require but the time *bodies* require. It admits the deep subjectivity of our experience of time—that we cannot simply measure time in minutes but by the length and strength of our legs and our arms.

Until the 2020 disruption of the "waking, quotidian world"[14] as I'd always known it, I lived the unquestioned assumptions of clock time. I cheered time management measures like efficiency and productivity. There wasn't anywhere to go just then, of course, but I was habituated to the dopamine hits of checking things off my list, then falling into bed at night.

By all accounts, I would have said I wanted to be less busy. As if from on high, I was granted reprieve by way of a global shutdown. But in this suddenly still season, when Jesus stood over the bow of my life, hushing the winds and the waves, the irony was this: I regretted the cease of the storm.

I wanted motion. Because I had always counted motion as meaning.

This motion we assume to be meaning—and this hegemony of the clock—ignores the value of people who move more slowly through the world. It creates barriers for the disabled and for the aging, even in our churches.[15] According to Hendren, for the sake of her son, Graham, and many others, we must do more than simply work to include the excluded. We have to reimagine a different kind of timekeeping. We have to *resist* the idea that to fail to move fast is to fall behind. "[Graham] needs a world with a robust countervailing understanding of personhood and contribution and community in it, human values that are alive and operational outside the logic of the market and its insistent clock," Hendren writes. "He needs it, and so do the rest of us."[16]

Better, Wiser Stories

We live by the stories we tell, even the stories we tell about time. Whether we realize it or not, we are mythmaking beings, always narrating the reality of the world and our place in it. Maybe the world is friendly or indifferent or hostile. Maybe we are good or depraved or improvable. Maybe we are alone here, and time is just another resource to economize, to exploit, to expend for our good pleasure. Or maybe the world is lovingly superintended by a Creator and Sustainer, a wise and good Giver of all things, including time itself.

Maybe we stand to learn the hours don't belong to us. And maybe a billboard, blinking the lesson in neon, won't be necessary after all.

On Living the Lord's Time

My friend Gwen came over yesterday afternoon and sat on my couch. She'd spent the summer day doing rounds at a local retirement home, where she works one day a week as a physician.

I didn't know Gwen well when we first began working together for *Imprint*, the literary arts magazine published by Grace Toronto Church. I was her editor for her first piece, a day-in-the-life of a family doctor. We'd titled it "Ordinary Time," and in it she'd written about her patients: nervous new mothers and older heartbroken ones. I also worked with Gwen more recently on a second piece, a meditation on her relationship with her aging mother. It had ended with the scene of her mother's death, who, after suffering dementia, had sat bolt upright in bed and exclaimed, "Hallelujah!"

On this hot August day, I make Gwen an iced coffee, then worry it is too watery. For the next hour, I confide in her this decision Ryan and I are considering: to move back to the States to support my aging mother. It's not the thing I want to do, I say, not when it means leaving the life we've built in Toronto for more than a decade—but it's the thing I can't seem to ignore.

"I suppose you must think, 'What choice do I have?'" she says sympathetically.

I nod vigorously—because this is exactly how I feel. My brother has been dead for more than twenty years. My mother has no siblings or cousins, my stepfather is ailing, and COVID has weakened their relational ties. In terms of the people my mother might reasonably rely on, there is mostly me: me with my freedom, me with my responsibility. I tell Gwen that it is as if God has led me to the sheer face of an immovable mountain, and while I don't want to climb it, I can't go around it either.

Toronto has become a city I love, a city I don't want to leave, and I can't help imagining what this choice will make of my life, my time. Will I make room in my busy life to be present for my mother in this way I now feel called? Can I make that room willingly?

I start to cry. I tell Gwen about the short stories I've been reading from the late Alexandros Papadiamandis, a writer who lamented, among other things, the individualism of modern life. His story "A Pilgrimage to Kastro" celebrates the collective action of seventeen villagers who brave the perils of winter winds and sail to rescue some stranded travelers.

Not everyone, of course, thinks this rescue mission is a good idea. "Every man's got to look after his own business," the character Panagos argues self-servingly. "Nobody's going to stick his head into the lion's mouth to save you."[1]

The village priest won't hear of any such self-preserving talk, and I try to paraphrase for Gwen his arguments for benevolence and self-sacrifice.

Christ has no need for people to go and celebrate the liturgy for him . . . but where there is a little good will, and one has a debt to pay, and maybe even if there is a risk involved where it has to do with helping others, as in our case here, there God comes to our side, even in the case of bad weather and a thousand obstacles . . . there God keeps us company, easing the way, working a miracle even.[2]

I tell Gwen I am sure of two things: the decision is hard, and I will count on God's help to do it, should it be necessary.

"We don't have to fear suffering, right?" I say. "Because isn't this when God is most near, most tender?"

This is something I want to believe. Or want to want to believe, as Gwen and I joke. I want to grab hold of the idea that this mountain looming ahead of me might be the very site of God's mercy, that if I make the climb, it will be cause for comfort. I tell Gwen how I want to abandon—or want to want to abandon—my death-wish for an invulnerable life, for time belonging solely to me, but I think of the struggle it is to make our way sometimes toward God's most spacious places.

I think of how easy it can be to procrastinate in matters of discipleship.

The call to resistance was always clear in the life of Israel. The nation was "chosen *from* the world" just as it was "equally chosen *for* the world."[3] Abraham and his people would become a blessing to the nations insofar as they preserved an identity of distinctiveness. The world was full of neighbors to love—not to imitate.

Because they were God's treasured possession, the sexual ethics of the Jews were different. Their customs of eating were different. On the Sabbath, Jews rested, and on the eighth day after birth, every Jewish boy was circumcised. These practices underlined the point about difference, about belonging. It underscored the call to resistance.

But Israel's difference was not simply encoded in the rules it followed. Their resistance was bound up in a story. It had a narrative arc. "I am the LORD your God, who brought you out of the land of Egypt, out of the house of slavery."[4]

This was the preamble to their most important law code, the ten words received by Moses at the summit of Mount Sinai. This preamble reminded them of the God they served and the rescue he effected. It reminded them of the freedom of true worship and the slavery of idolatry. To have remained in Egypt would have been to remain victim to the inhumane logic of productivity. In Egypt, they were the makers of bricks—machines in the national economy. But as God's people, called to be his, they were instead freed to flourish in ways unimagined. They were freed to be still and know that God was God. They were freed to resist, even to rest.

If we're honest with ourselves, we can admit this freedom—to rest, to be still—is one we have rarely known in the "seculosity" of modern life. As David Zahl describes in his book by that title, parenting, exercise, romantic pursuits, and political commitments today demand a kind of strenuous effort to prove we are *enough*. They are measures of morality, forms of small-*r* religion, things we lean on to "tell us we're okay, that our lives matter."[5] Busyness is, in and of itself, one crucial means of self-justification, according to Zahl. We run to escape the silence of slowing down and the questions that might linger there, in the noiselessness.

It's no exaggeration to say that the dictates of time management function like the commands of a false god. The logic of productivity dehumanizes, as idolatry always does. Make widgets, and make them faster, *faster!* "Those who make [idols] become like them; so do all who trust in them."[6] But though we may recognize the truth of this, acts of resistance, even resistance to our own demise, don't come easy, especially when we're constantly judged by our CVs. Who can slow down when there is so much to prove?

It takes courage to decide to keep the hours differently and receive a different kind of life. And here is the truth of my own life: courage is often something I lack.

Time management books would keep our heads bowed over the minutes of our days. They would have us counting the time that ticks, that elapses, that marches on. They would keep us believing we're falling behind, that hurry—no matter its irritability—is necessary and needful. But the Christian story, in resistance to this kind of spiritual myopia, reminds us that there is more to making a life than keeping the hours productively and efficiently. The Christian story lifts our eyes to the *mountains,* to the Maker of heaven and earth.

"My help comes from the LORD. . . . The LORD will keep your going out and your coming in from this time forth and forevermore."[7] It's this help I am going to count on if God says *Climb.*

Higher Time

I've moved more times than I can count—and that may be the real conundrum of the decision ahead of us, that it involves another leaving, another going. I've longed for permanence, but like sand, it keeps slipping through my fingers.

I've written a lot about my serial moving and the experience of myself as a drifter.[8] I've thought of myself as someone like Sylvie, the unstable aunt in Marilynne Robinson's novel *Housekeeping*, conscripted to care for her young nieces after the death of their mother and grandmother. Sylvie had the habit of sleeping on top of the covers with her shoes on. She kept her personal effects stowed in a cardboard box beneath the bed.

Most of us know something of the experience of modern mobility and what it means to live less tethered to our places than previous generations. My hunch is that, in the absence of geographical stability, *time* has been substituted for *place* as the dominant context of modern life. If, as the apostle Paul says in Acts 17, God has determined both the "periods" of our lives and the "boundaries of [our] dwelling place,"[9] today we seem to have far more consciousness of the former than the latter.

We don't recognize we're rootless now, only that we are pressed for time.

Today is the first day that I bother to look up the Greek word for "periods," as it is translated in the English Standard Version. I discover that the word is *kairos*. It is the word for time that differs from *chronos*, from which we derive words such as chronology. *Kairos* is not the time we keep with our watches, which is, of course, a more historically recent understanding of time. *Kairos* is not the time we count as money, not the thing we save or spend or waste or lose. *Kairos* reminds us that there is a mode of time that exists beyond the curtain of a day, beyond the veil of a life.[10] And while there isn't always a neat distinction in the New Testament between these words that would allow us to construct a systematic theology of time, it's certainly true that the biblical writers granted a kind of time the productivity experts don't know how to measure.

In *A Secular Age*, Charles Taylor recounts the story of the last five hundred years, when we began to tell time differently. In part, the "secular" story is how all time became ordinary time. According to Taylor, since AD 1500, a shifting conception of time has given way to a rise in what Taylor calls "exclusive humanism." This brave, new, modern world of ours has been drained of transcendent, otherworldly purpose. We don't grant the existence of God, much less our obligations to him. Today, the only time we owe is to ourselves: to our careers, to our picture-perfect families, to our bucket lists. This accounts, in large part, for our time devotedness—or should we say time greed? Because if time is money . . .

Just as there once was sacred space (in medieval cathedrals, for example), there was also sacred time. In fact, prior to the Reformation, we looked to the monks and nuns to renounce earthly pleasures and commit themselves to prayer. They lived the Lord's time for the rest of us. By contrast, few people try living the Lord's time today. What we're left with instead is successive moments that "we try to measure and control in order to get things done."[11] If all time is ordinary time, it is all subject to the goals (and goads) of productivity.

To keep the hours Christianly, we must recover habits of higher time. And that's my intention in this book: to explore the nature of living in time more faithfully, more joyfully, more hopefully. The habits of higher time don't have much to do with traditional time management advice—its tips and tricks, its techniques and tools. I don't discount the help I've received from many of the books I've read, but I do suspect the campaign promises of getting things done.

There is an important difference between improved executive functioning and time faith.

Habits of higher time have little to do with time savvy. Calendaring may be involved, but mostly these habits involve a "labor of vision," to borrow a phrase from another writer.[12] Because, despite our best efforts at productivity, our lives will fog, then evaporate, like winter breath. We will die. As the prophet Isaiah reminds us, "All flesh is grass, and all its beauty is like the flower of the field."[13] We will not finish all we've begun, will not accomplish all we've intended. Life will chill, the days will shorten, and our bodies will catch in death's wind and fall like autumn leaves. *Dust to dust.* We will get no second chances on mortal time and its gifts.

If we fail to see time stretching beyond the final shudder of this life, beyond the final slow wheeze of earthly breath, we are people to be pitied. Jesus told a story about a man like this, a man without appreciation of eternity. He was a man whose entire life had been so absolutely devoted to the accumulation of wealth that he'd postponed even the pleasures of enjoying it. After he finally entered the golden years of retirement, putting up his feet poolside somewhere in south Florida, he stretched out his hand to seize his first moment of peace: "Soul, you have ample goods laid up for many years; relax, eat, drink, be merry."[14]

That man, Jesus said, was a fool. He didn't know the measure of time, didn't know in the scope of mortal life what would suffer loss—and what would last.

This book involves unlearning: about time as instrument, about time as material aspiration. Its project is one that involves the slow growth of wisdom. It will invite each of us into a different imagining of time, which is to say the generous sweep of heavenly time, where God's will is being done without delay or haste. In this world, rather indifferent to the urgent ticking of the clock, we are free to be still, free to be small, free to take refuge in the one who was and is and ever will be God.

Growing Time

On the one hand, I'm well suited to the task I am giving to myself in these pages ahead. It's not just that I'm a recovering time manager, someone who has come to see as fraudulent all the promises of bottling time and pouring it at will. I'm a Christian, someone who is discovering how the arc of the biblical story teaches us to tell time. And, if I am to believe the actuarial tables, I am also squarely in the middle of life. Perhaps this is to say that I'm more sobered about the power of personal ambition, more tempered by life's intractable realities. Given that I am graying, I am growing more and more committed to finishing well.

Disappointingly to some, perhaps, I'm neither a philosopher nor a scholar, and despite having watched several videos about the theory of relativity, I am still incapable of explaining it. But while I can't engage the most abstract questions of time, can't even pretend to have read all the ponderous sections on time in Augustine's *Confessions*, I can, perhaps, as a writer, lead us into a kind of Wood between the Worlds, like Digory and Polly find in *The Magician's Nephew*. There, we can almost feel the trees drinking up water by their roots. There, the world is quiet and still, and in the shade of those trees, we grow convinced there is far less need for hurry. It will take imagination—which is to say, faith—to believe in that world. I, myself, am only just beginning.

I confess there isn't much I know about trees, though I've grown fascinated by them in Scripture this last year. Trees grow up in the middle of the Bible's most important stories, and they help us picture what it means to live the Lord's time and produce perpetual fruit. Like other biblical writers, the prophet Jeremiah draws a marvelous contrast between the wise man and the foolish man, the first as a well-watered tree, the second as a desert shrub. "Cursed is the man who trusts in man and makes flesh his strength, whose heart turns away from the LORD. . . . Blessed is the man who trusts in the LORD, whose trust is in the LORD."[15]

Living in Toronto's midtown, I'm grateful to have even a small yard and a row of beech trees growing along the backyard fence. I've never lived long enough in one place to watch trees grow, but as this was our second spring in this house, a house we'd moved into just months before the pandemic, I knew at the very least to expect that the rest of the yard would burst into bloom before my beech trees.

Trees are a product of time. Time is required for seeing trees rooted deep and standing tall. And that's ultimately what my interest is, in this book and in my life. I wonder about the robed and radiant beauty of God's people, patiently living the Lord's time and believing in its plenty.

These last couple of years, with their inwardness and isolation, have shifted something in me. I want, at first, to write the word *seismic* to describe the change, but that would be imprecise and would suggest an earthquake. This is not the way that God often comes to his people, as we know from the story of Elijah. The prophet looks for God in the earthquake, in the fire, in the strong wind. But God speaks with a whisper, and there has to be a stillness—a leaning in—to hear.

In recent months, the virus has waxed and waned. I have grown busy again. Some days, I have been anxious. But something has been different too. I'm less hungry for motion, less convinced that's where meaning is found. I want to discover—or want to want to discover—the endless time plenty hidden in the God who is without beginning or end.

The good and wise Giver of days.

PART 2

ON TIME FAITH

HABIT 1

Begin

As we tell the true story of time, we seize the hope we can begin—and begin again.

In March 2020, I drafted a list of the things our family would do during our two-week quarantine after we arrived home from our beach vacation. We would read together. We would memorize Scripture. We would clean out closets and check in daily with our extended family back in the States. I would finish the manuscript of another book, then continue work on the rule of life I'd begun drafting in the early mornings before sunrise, the ocean as soundtrack. I had been up early each day that week at the beach to hammer out a version of monastic timekeeping and decide—in advance—how to spend the days of my life.

I am a sucker for beginnings. The resolve of January. The turn of September and its launch into another school year.

I love the pages of a new planner—when time is sloughed off and soon to be regenerated. A beginning can act like an overture. You start to dream of the new start you'll make in your career, your most important relationships, your daily schedule, your spiritual life.

In the broad sweep of time, a beginning can signal hope.

Time management, as an industry, is poised on the consumer promise of beginnings. That moment when your messy life is as neatly ordered as a Marie Kondo drawer of shirts standing on end? It is just around the corner. It will only take a conference or retreat, an online course or better digital system, to achieve it. And of course, according to all the time management experts, beginnings are ripe occasion for lists. Making lists is one habit of productive people. They don't leave their days—even pandemic days—to chance. They have three choices in life: "drift, drown, or decide."[1]

In the beginning of this new pandemic world, I decided to decide.

None of us knew, of course, that the public health crisis would outlast our personal ambition. We did not know in March 2020, when the borders of countries closed and businesses, schools, restaurants, salons, and gyms shuttered, that this would be more than an interruption to the regularly scheduled broadcast of our lives. We were dumped blindfolded into unmapped territory—and we stayed longer at this beginning than planned.

In the fall of 2021, I verify some of the estimates of devastation from the CDC: 120.1 million total infections, 101.8 million symptomatic illnesses, 6.2 million hospitalizations, 767,000 total deaths.[2]

Falsely, time management assures us it is always ours to *decide*. And while I want to believe I can throw my shoulder at the hulk of this day, forcing it to open to me, as we've learned the last couple of years, such power is not always possible on our infected planet. Yes, the business of wisdom calls us to the responsibility of deciding. But sometimes our deciding is impotent. Sometimes reality resists change. Sometimes, despite our best efforts, we don't avoid disaster. We like to believe we're managers of time, but we must also admit we're often its victims.

To consider what 2020 launched all of us into is to think of the root meaning of the word *germ*, which Eula Biss notes in her book *On Immunity*. "We use the same word for something that brings illness and something that brings growth. The root of the word being, of course, *seed*."[3]

Perhaps it's best to say that in mortal time, beginnings are complicated. Germs and seeds, in other words. Sometimes a beginning is the dawning of morning light. And sometimes a beginning is the door we grope for in the dark.

According to the Bible, God is the first—and only infallible—Beginner. When the world was "welter and waste and darkness over the deep,"[4] God caused new realities to rise up out of emptiness. Let there be light! Let there be birds! Let there be savannas and zebras, oceans and blue whales! God spoke, and a beginning took shape. Time itself was a part of God's good creation.

Genesis, our first book of the Bible, is a catalog of these beginnings, and at first glance, their tenor is bravado. As evening is separated from morning, as water is separated from sky, as human beings are sculpted from soil and bone, our stories of beginning speak fundamental truths about reality: love and order, not rivalry and chaos, have founded the world. In the beginning is God, Maker and sharer of his own image. These first stories are birth stories, stories to tell us how God labored to deliver the world. They have long been evidence for God's power to produce a beginning.

But to read further in the book of Genesis is to discover just how complicated beginnings can turn out to be. It seems, in fact, that beginnings, in the hands of human beings, can be fumbled like a football. God births this teeming world of light and love—and that world suffers great grief only three chapters into the story. Human beings abuse the freedom they've been given and are exiled from the very good garden God has made as their home.

God begins—and God's people don't carry his beginnings very far.

According to Hebrew scholar Robert Alter, there is a literary observation to be made about many of the beginnings detailed in the book of Genesis, especially those that launch with Abraham in chapter 12. We should be astonished, Alter explains, that the majority of the Old Testament is written in prose. Other ancient religions favored myth and legend and epic poetry for theological texts.[5] Myth and legend support a view of reality where God enacts "cosmic events in the manner of sympathetic magic." What myth and legend don't support are the complications of beginnings; instead, they get beginnings done.

The prose of the Bible, by contrast, testifies to a different kind of time, one that doesn't travel as imperiously from Point A to Point B. It's a story that testifies to God's providence, yes, but also to the ambiguities of the human condition. Prose allows the biblical writers to maintain the tension between "the divine promise and its ostensible failure to be fulfilled." Prose allows for a record of the human actor "created by an all-seeing God but abandoned to his or her own unfathomable freedom, made in God's likeness . . . but almost never as a matter of accomplished ethical fact."[6] Only prose can give us figures like Jacob, who cheated his brother out of his blessing and yet bore the name of God's people.

Only prose can feature time and its many human fumbles.

To think of where Genesis ends—Joseph, dead and buried in Egypt—is to wonder about God's power to make good on what he's begun. What of all those promises to Abraham, of land and family and nationhood? Had Genesis been written as myth or legend, we might not worry after God's beginnings and his capacity to make *everything good in its time*. But as it's written, Genesis seems to suggest that while God acts providently in history, at any point in time, the story can have a harrowed quality to it. You might begin with bravado, with ambition, and many months or years later, find yourself a little lost.

A beginning might look like a baby tangled in an umbilical cord, head down and stuck. Sometimes you wait for a beginning in an operating room, listening for a heartbeat. You're glad for one of the doctors squeezing your shoulder and saying it's going to be okay.

Trouble, Trouble

I was delivered into my mother's arms on Mother's Day, at Elkhart General Hospital, in 1974. "The best gift I ever received," my mom likes to say. Every time, she recalls the minute: 3:14 a.m.

"What time was I born?" my own children have asked. I remember Audrey came midafternoon on a Wednesday, the day before my scheduled induction and the day after my mother and I had eaten lunch at Panda Express. The night before Nathan was born, I remember eating dinner with the neighbors and putting Audrey to bed with a wheezy cough. A year and a half later, I remember lumbering to TCBY at dusk on a Friday, my belly sagging low with Camille. Hours later, when we arrived at the hospital and they measured my cervix, I was warned by an unsympathetic nurse I might be sent home. Ryan and I lapped the halls, and sometime before 9:00 a.m., our second daughter—the one with the dimpled cheek—was laid in my arms.

Three years later, I delivered twins. I remember spending the last months of that pregnancy stretched in front of the *PBS News Hour* with Jim Lehrer, nursing a sore back and tired legs. Two weeks after Barack Obama's upset in the Iowa Caucuses, on January 19, "Baby A" was delivered first in a fit of my laughter. "Hold on a second!" my doctor said, pulling on his gloves. "Baby B" hung on another hour. He was finally delivered by C-section, emerging as if tangled in wires, the umbilical cord wrapped around his waist and looped over his shoulder; he was squeezing it like a morphine drip. "I thought of you all day yesterday," my doctor said on his rounds. "Those two babies were both head-down. I thought for sure we'd have no trouble."

That cold and snowy day in January 2008, the doctor expected no trouble. He predicted a beginning, delivered without complication. And isn't that what we all want? Time as untroubled waters? Maybe Christians want this most, given that we affirm God's mastery over time. If he can calm the wind and waves, what can he not do with hours and years?

The book that was a cult classic among my stay-at-home-mother set in my evangelical church when Audrey was a baby was *Growing Kids God's Way*. It was the kind of book that promised to wind babies like clocks, to teach them to mind clinical schedules for napping and nursing and lying contentedly awake. To read this book was to be assured that there was one divinely ordained—and presumably foolproof—way to raise children. At the time, I wanted nothing more than hot cups of coffee. I wanted to shower at will and believe the baby could be left to coo quietly in her crib before the imaginary whistle. I wanted to know my children would be good. "That's not a book I'd recommend," another mother warned. She had a ten-year-old, and it lent her an air of expertise.

I didn't read the book. Maybe I knew I could not be trusted with such presumptions of power, such ham-fisted certainties. Maybe I was spared, by grace, the brute force of my own autocratic desires. And still, there's no doubt I continued clinging tightly to illusions of control, just as Colin clung for life to that umbilical cord. I worked hard to be a diligent, devoted mother—diligence and devotion having power, I believed, to head trouble off at the pass.

But it came for us. Trouble, that is. For our family, trouble came during our long season of burrowing pandemic isolation. To be clear, we did not suffer the kind of crisis many families with teenagers have. (To date, three of our closest friends have hospitalized their children with suicidal ideation and severe depression since the beginning of the pandemic.) Let me simply say that one Saturday morning I went looking for a child's shoe and found—to borrow from Julian of Norwich—a showing. One shoe, missing then recovered in the backyard, led to a host of discoveries: namely, that one of my children had been lying to me for months, and that the lying was meant to cover up worse offenses.

That morning, I discovered trouble was not to be bullied by me.

I had cherished memories of all our children's baptisms. I believed each baptism signaled an important beginning, begun not by me, not by Ryan, but by God himself. "Baptism is a promise," our pastor always says, when he sprinkles water on the heads of unsuspecting babies. "Not a guarantee, but an invitation held out." I believed in that water, and I could rehearse truths about God's everlasting faithfulness. I knew his steadfast love was long, for his friends and their children. But after I found the shoe and suffered that midnight betrayal, after I remembered the years of innocence and recalled that broken bond of trust, I also knew what it meant to wonder how the beginning went wrong.

Time for Hope

"One day, he just said, 'I don't love you anymore,'" my friend tells me of her recent divorce. Her husband had gathered twenty years of marriage like kindling and lit them with a match. She tugs at her ponytail, wipes her face with the back of her hand—and as we walk in the afternoon rain, I'm faced again with the question of beginnings. Questions of trouble, and this telling of higher time.

At some point we're all left to wonder, Just how far can we trust God's promise of *all things working for good*? The prophet Isaiah figured humanity as a cloud of grasshoppers, with lives small and brief. In contrast, he cited God's eternal power as a primordial Beginner: "Lift up your eyes on high and see: who created these? He who brings out their host by number, calling them all by name: by the greatness of his might and because he is strong in power, not one is missing."[7] The prophet affirmed all this, in response to a question we might all have asked, especially in times of trouble: "Why do you say, O Jacob, and speak, O Israel, 'My way is hidden from the LORD, and my right is disregarded by my God?'"[8] To walk through the valley of the shadow of death is to sometimes suspect God has left a beginning to burn like forgotten pancakes.

Trouble begs us to make meaning—and to tell meaningful stories about time. On the one hand, I believe in Christ, risen from the dead. This is to say that I believe in beginnings. God's business is new things, and he cuts roads through deserts and rivers through wastelands. This is a promise to hold to when it seems we've run into what seems to be time's dead end. On the other hand, I know enough to understand that life can rupture along a fault line. In this life, not everything gets repaired. Time can wound, and we can bleed.

I was seventeen when I found a folded letter on my bed from my father. The impression I had then was of his words crossing a gaping, glassy silence. Of words having traveled a great distance or echoed from some remote cave. "I haven't taken time lately to sit down and write," the letter began. I saved those three pages torn from his yellow legal pad, the same pad of pages where he composed poems for my mother on occasions like her birthday or their anniversary. Short, staccato verses. Every line ending in a dash. Every stanza reading like a list: "Jan, you are my wife, my friend, my companion—" I didn't believe those verses then, not for the paper, not for the form. But those three yellow pages scrawled to me months before my high school graduation? They had weight. I couldn't know he'd be dead in a year, proving how quickly a life can wither and fade, between a morning cup of coffee and the time it takes to warm the car.

My own mother has lost not just a husband but also a son—her only son, by his own hand. *O my son Absalom, O Absalom, my son, my son!*[9] She tells me later this is the verse she wailed aloud in her car for the better part of a year, driving to and from work, after his death. What to say of beginnings when you've come home from a weekend away and, while lugging your suitcases through the garage, found your son bent over the wheel of your car? *O my son Absalom, O Absalom, my son, my son!* What to say of beginnings when you've touched your son's shoulder and found it cold? I was sitting beside my mother when the funeral director told her it would be inadvisable to try to see him one last time. He pushed a small plastic bag toward us from his side of the table and called it "effects." I know another truth about beginnings, that they can be smothered like a sob.

I am getting used to how implausible faith in beginnings can sound. There is a certain savageness to a world of rising seas and raging wildfires, stillborn babies, and incurable cancers. There is a savageness to a world of global pandemics and mutating viruses, racial trauma and political violence. In 1947, Martyl Langsdorf designed, for publication in the *Bulletin of Atomic Scientists,* "The Clock of Doom."[10] It was a clock meant for keeping a particular kind of anxious time—the time until nuclear war.

In 1947, the clock was set at seven minutes to midnight. On January 23, 2020, its hands were moved to one hundred seconds to midnight, signaling what we all know: that it is a broken world we inhabit, and no one is invulnerable. "Immunity is a myth," writes Eula Biss, "and no mortal can ever be made invulnerable."[11] This seems to be the truth that the prose of Genesis bears witness to: to live outside of the Garden is to suffer the looming possibility of trouble.

I've said I believe in beginnings. As a Christian, I must. What is Christ raised from the dead if not a beginning? What is Christ ascended and returning if not a promise of what's yet to come? And still, life is heavy with loss—pregnant with it, we might say. There is always this lurking fear that while we insist on the constancy of God, we will get gravel instead.

We do not know why suffering is meted out so randomly in the world, why some get beginnings in this mortal life and others don't. But maybe the fierce insistence on the power and possibility of beginnings is a stubborn habit of hope. As theologian N. T. Wright has put it, hope is not to be confused with naïve optimism.

"The optimist looks at the world," he writes,

> and feels good about the way it's going. . . . But hope, at least as conceived within the Jewish and then the early Christian world, was quite different. Hope could be, and often was, a dogged and deliberate choice when the world seemed dark. It depended not on a *feeling* about the way things were or the way they were moving, but on *faith*, faith in the One God.[12]

Hope, in other words, is not glib or cloying or falsely reassuring. It can admit the reality of trouble. It can grieve and lament and wail. It can shake its fist at the heavens, all while stubbornly clinging to faith. Wright explains further:

> [Hope] is a virtue. You have to practice it, like a difficult piece on the violin or a tricky shot at tennis. You practice the virtue of hope through worship and prayer, through invoking the One God, through reading and reimagining the scriptural story, and through consciously holding the unknown future within the unshakeable divine promises.[13]

Hope, as a habit of higher time, has a certain orientation to the past. It's the habit of rehearsing what God has already done, what God has already promised. In the beginning, God created the world for the sake of love. When it faltered and fell, he promised redemption through one tiny seed.

Hope is also oriented toward the future. It looks beyond this here-and-now world groaning as if in the pains of childbirth. It tells us this world's trouble, however long, however tenacious, however dark, isn't to be compared to the glory to come. For Christians, the arc of our story isn't beginning, middle, and end. In Christ, our story begins and begins again.

If you only live once, your hope lasts only as long as this life. But if your life can be incorporated into the God who makes all things new, if you can hold to the vision of Revelation 21 of a world from which mourning and pain have passed away, you have time for hope.

"We do not know why God delays so long," Fleming Rutledge admits in her book on Advent, this season of the church calendar dedicated to hope.

> We do not know why he so often hides his face. We do not know why so many have to suffer so much with so little apparent meaning. All we know is that there is this rumor, this hope, this expectation that the Master of the house is coming back.[14]

Hope is what holds us up between time's contractions.

My Bible reading took me recently through the book of Job, and I was grateful to have my new copy of Robert Alter's translation and commentary. In the first chapter, I couldn't help but see the "immunity" Job sought on behalf of his children, offering sacrifices for the sins they may have committed. "For Job thought, Perhaps my sons have offended and cursed God in their hearts."[15]

It is not fifteen verses later that they're all dead, struck by a great wind that has collapsed the house around them in the middle of a family feast. For the bulk of the book, Job rails against the perceived injustice of his suffering, and although he never gets answers, he does finally get a beginning: more children and restored health and prosperity.

Alter tells readers that the book is a work of masterful poetry. He insists, however, that the "greater poetry" is reserved for God, who answers Job from the whirlwind. "Who is this who darkens counsel in words without knowledge?"[16] Knowledge is what we often lack when trying to trace some solid line between cause and event, between beginning and hope, between missing shoe and solid ground. Suffering has a way of eroding all our pieties and platitudes.

When the time of trouble comes, it can—if we let it— give birth to hope.

Because when the world turns to us its coldest shoulder, we are never abandoned. God did not consider immunity a thing to be grasped but made himself nothing, taking the vulnerable form of a crowning baby and crucified King.

This is what I try to remind my friend grieving in the wake of her divorce. It is what I try to remember myself in the weeks after the shoe, the showing, and the lying awake. The hope of the gospel does not mean denying evil but expecting its defeat. It does not mean pretending away grief or neglecting lament but craning our necks to glimpse the horizon of a new day.

If Christ is the incarnate beginning, it must be true that God is never as impatient as we are to close a case, to call it a wrap, to declare a thing ended. In this strange world we call the kingdom, God can lean over dead things—and find a pulse.

Ready for a Baptism

Our friends are climbing the stairs for the baptism of their daughter. The father is carrying his long-legged little girl in his arms. The mother is trailing behind in a long dress. I miss these friends, friends I haven't seen much of during the church's long shuttering.

This daughter they are baptizing has her own story of beginning. She has come to these parents after a long season of many sufferings, and now she is finally being introduced to the congregation as she receives the waters of grace. I see her hair, banded in small knots, and remember that God does indeed answer prayer, that God can indeed grant beginnings when we ask.

Our pastor gives our friends their charge as parents: to unreservedly dedicate this child to God, and to promise, in humble reliance upon divine grace, that they will endeavor to set before her a godly example, that they will pray for her, that they will teach her the doctrines of our holy religion, and that they will strive, by all the means of God's appointment, to bring her up in the nurture and admonition of the Lord. The words remind me of my own parenting task, with which I've felt burdened in recent months.

In the weeks after my child's shoe went missing—and with it, trust—I began reading Julian of Norwich. I learned her visionary text was passed hand to hand after it was written by the medieval anchorite, manuscripts copied and recopied by Benedictine French nuns over the centuries before its first printing in 1670. As far as scholars can tell, the book never reached the broad readership Julian might have wanted, perhaps because it was written by "a simple creature unlettered." In my mind's eye, it was a clap of miracle that *A Revelation of Love* should arrive in my hands, more than six centuries later, at my hour of need.

Julian's revelation of love—a vivid showing of the crucified Christ—comes to her as a suffering she has summoned. She has longed for woundedness: as participation in the sufferings of Christ, as a penitence and purgation, as one way by which she might be made to desire God. Julian wills herself bruised—and God grants Julian her desire when, for three days and three nights, she lies dying. From her deathbed, she sees a crucifix grow suddenly luminous. Jesus's brow, crowned with thorns, is bleeding.

In her vision, Julian sees the open side of Christ like the breast of a nursing mother. To her, it is a picture of God's generous self-giving, God's unbounded hospitality, God's unwearied love. She sees that God's self-sacrifice has cost God no real difficulty, no real sense of expenditure. Christ would be broken open, again and again, to feed us, and it would never be resentment for him.

Scholars have called Julian's text an "affective theology." This is to say that it is not meant to fill our minds with theological truths. Rather, as Jacqueline Jenkins puts it in her introduction, it is a work that acts "as an answer to human need."[17] I will admit that, as I read, Julian does not convince me entirely that Jesus is the source of human motherhood and mother himself to the human race, which is central to her revelation. But when I open this text in the weeks following that Saturday morning shoe discovery, I find this is exactly who I need Jesus to be. These are weeks I live between worry and waking, weeks I want to be wound and wrapped in Christ himself. I wonder if God will subvert, as promised, his ancient law: "In those days they shall no longer say: 'The fathers have eaten sour grapes, and the children's teeth are set on edge.'"[18] I worry that I've somehow caused this trouble with my child by the spectacular failures of my parenting.

This image of Julian's mother-Christ helped me begin again as a mother with my child. I fed at the bleeding side of Christ, this Man of Sorrows pierced for transgressions, crushed for every sin and trouble. I began to forgive.

I take so much comfort that Paul says, over and over again in his letters, that beginnings are possible. To put your faith in Christ, the "firstborn from the dead,"[19] is to join the ranks of the resurrected. The reborn. To the Galatians: "For neither circumcision counts for anything, nor uncircumcision, but a new creation."[20] To the Corinthians: "Therefore, if anyone is in Christ, he is a new creation. The old has passed away; behold, the new has come."[21] To the Ephesians: "But God, being rich in mercy, because of the great love with which he loved us, even when we were dead in our trespasses, made us alive together with Christ."[22] To the Colossians: "Put on the new self, which is being renewed in knowledge after the image of its creator."[23]

Whoever enters the waters of baptism, as I did at age nine, is not the same person to leave them. Baptism blinks in neon: mercy is powerful. Conversion is possible. The record of trespass and debt has been canceled, and "there is therefore now no condemnation for those who are in Christ Jesus."[24]

When you've come to an end of yourself and recognized you can't do better, try harder, or make amends; when you've acknowledged your need not just for improvement but complete rehabilitation—or when your parents have acknowledged this on your behalf—you're ready for a baptism.

You're ready for a beginning.

At six, I knelt beside the bed with my mother in Kent, Ohio, and "asked Jesus to come into my heart." I knew I was a sinner, that Jesus was someone to "trust and obey." At nine, I was baptized in the towering baptistry of First Baptist Church in Jackson, Tennessee, backdropped by stained glass. At sixteen, I stood beside a lake at Seneca Lake Baptist Assembly and heard the voice of Jesus as if for the very first time: *What do you want? Where are you headed? Will you follow?*

Sometimes I wonder, Just how many beginnings can God grant in one life?

Skipping like a Stone

Maybe beginnings are the narrative device we choose to tell our own stories in time—to tell them with hope.

I open my Bible reading this morning to the first chapter of 1 Chronicles. Inwardly, I sigh. *The genealogies.* This is not the portion of Scripture you count on to rouse yourself from sleep and shake off a weekend of eating fast food, hauling boxes up and down stairs, spending long hours in the car, and fighting traffic. It is not the pick-me-up you need after helping your oldest children move into their college apartment.

I am tired, but I give this beginning—this *begetting*—in 1 Chronicles a try. I notice, in the first verse, the names that have been left out of the first human family: "The descendants of Adam were Seth, Enosh, Kenan, Mahalalel, Jared, Enoch, Methuselah, Lamech, and Noah."[25] This chronicler of Israel's history has begun selectively, omitting Cain and Abel, the first sons of Adam.

I pull down a commentary from my shelf and read that this book, telling much of what 1 and 2 Samuel and 1 and 2 Kings also tell, presents Israel's monarchical history differently.

> The differences, the distinctive features of Chronicles, have to do with the Chronicler's theology—truths about God and the people of God are his special concern. He assumes throughout that his readers know the facts already, and his object is to interpret them.[26]

This beginning, then, is telling a certain kind of story. It's freighted with meaning.

I read that Chronicles was written after Israel's return from exile. This historical moment represented a beginning again for the nation, and the history of this chronicler "speaks of the possibility of its reunification and renewal."[27] Israel has suffered for its rebellion against God and has been dispossessed of the land he granted them. When they eventually return, they come home to broken walls and a razed temple.

The temple is eventually rebuilt, but it's a sham copy of the first. As a result, there is rejoicing—and weeping—at the very same time.

> All the people shouted with a great shout when they praised the LORD, because the foundation of the house of the LORD was laid. But many of the priests and Levites

and heads of fathers' houses, old men who had seen the first house, wept with a loud voice.[28]

The young counted this building—this beginning—as hope. The old, on the other hand, required more faith.

And this is what I've been trying to say here, about beginnings. Sometimes we recognize them—and sometimes we leap into them unaware. Sometimes a beginning has the visible fingerprints of God—and sometimes a beginning is the moment the lights go out. Sometimes a beginning starts as storm—and in that storm, you remember you're sheltered and safe. Underneath is "the Rock that bore you . . . the God who gave you birth."[29]

In some cases, beginnings can indeed arrive like a baby: gestated, delivered, swaddled in hope. You decorate for a beginning, put a stork in the yard. And sometimes a beginning is the first night you spend away from home, shivering from the cold. Tomorrow is an unpredictable thing, as the biblical writers knew. But today, in this morning of life, God's mercies are made new.

"Few phrases are more significant than 'in the beginning,'" theologian Stanley Hauerwas writes.[30] And it does seem that the biblical story is particularly fond of beginnings. To think of all the gospel movement between Genesis and John, between John and Revelation, is to notice how God is in the business of fresh starts.

It's to see that from beginning to beginning to beginning, the story of God skips like a stone.

I think of this when my friend, whose daughter has just been baptized, texts me a picture of her daughter propped in a crease on the couch. "This is her bored teenager look," my friend says. I think of that doctor in the operating room on the January morning I delivered twins. He'd been late to pull on his gloves, sure that there would be no trouble. Trouble is not something to be predicted—but trouble isn't the only thing to see.

There's got to be a beginning in here somewhere.

TO CONSIDER

What beginnings have marked important moments in your own life, especially your life with God?

Have any of those beginnings faltered?

What hope, what courage, what faith, what wisdom might you ask God to renew by his grace?

TO PRAY

God, you are the one who begins, sustains, and begins again. In the pain and perplexity of this life, I easily lose my place in time. Help me to be nourished by the hope of Christ, your incarnate beginning. In this day, in this season, do a new thing, do it by your grace, and let me see it and participate in it. I believe in your unfaltering, eternal promises, and I hope in your everlasting day.

Receive

As we learn our limits, we abandon the impulse to manage
time and, instead, embrace the hours as a gift.

Call it your Coronavirus diary, your plague journal,
whatever. It's important. Later, you will want a record."[1]

It's not until April 4, 2020, that I record my first case
counts—3,836 in Chicago, 986 in Toronto—in my journal.
It's also the first day I copy headlines: "CDC Recommends
Wearing Cloth Masks in Public" and "Ferrets, Hamsters
Will Soon Reveal Whether Canadian Vaccine Bid Has a
Shot." We are almost a month into the global crisis, and
I feel as if we have been turned inside like monks, like
nuns—like a mother with a nursing newborn.

I describe it like this in a poem I write months later for
a writing workshop:

> unprecedented times, they say
> to suggest the unfamiliar.

but I know this narrowed view of things,
the world constricting, confining
growing small and interior.
every drama, quotidian.
every emergency, underfoot.
I know the feel of Thursday without ever leaving
the house.

In the *before* era, when life had the dizzying motion of a Tilt-A-Whirl, I'd make my coffee early in the morning and hole up in my basement office behind a closed door. I'd pray—and find it easy, in my office, to cut prayer short.

In this new era, I change my location after I wake up. Maybe I need reassuring signs of life that I can glimpse from my front window. In the pages of my new journal, I begin archiving a world we don't recognize and yet find ourselves receiving. *Today, Ryan and I are expecting a delivery of our garage organization supplies.* The world becomes something to carry in from the front porch, something delivered by strange people speeding in unmarked vans.

March 17, 2020: I am managing a decent amount of productivity. It's also true I am subject to near constant interruption.

March 26: One important thing to continue thinking through is: goals, ambitions, and desires.

March 29: I feel myself hurrying through the pandemic prayers I published. I've been at them for nearly two weeks.

April 2: The grocery bill was eye-popping. We're buying for Constance and her family too.

April 7: Yesterday was a day of unusual momentum, energy, and discipline. I have been rereading productivity books and reorganizing my lists.

April 9: Hilary, from the salon, dropped off a home hair color kit.

April 12: We waited forty-five minutes to carry out from Chick-fil-A. The line was maybe fifteen people deep.

My "plague" journal becomes hundreds of pages of observations where I catalog change and also sameness. My hurry and my hustle, it seems, are hard habits to break.

I was sixteen when I began keeping early morning hours with God. At the end of the weeklong Christian youth camp where I *decided to follow Jesus*, I was told my sapling faith was a fragile thing, that it would need to be sustained by ordinary habits. These were helpfully quantified for someone who likes to do things right. I'd need ten minutes every day in the Bible, five minutes every day for prayer, and at least once each week I'd need to tell someone else about Jesus.

I liked those rules, and I made promises to keep them for the next six months. I was so scrupulous in keeping those promises that on the summer morning I slept over at a friend's house and we woke up early to drive two hours to Six Flags, I asked her drowsily, "Want to read the Bible with me?" It didn't matter that she wasn't a Christian. I was not missing a day.

If I lived according to *The Rule of Saint Benedict*, which I began reading in the early months of 2020, I wouldn't simply have been up early to pray. I would have also slept with my clothes on. When the prayer bell rang in the middle of the night, I would have relied on the encouragement of my brothers or sisters, understanding that "the sleepy like to make excuses."[2]

Prayer was central to daily life within the Benedictine monastery. In fact, as Benedict understood it, there was less marked difference between prayer and work in the monastery. Prayer was work—and work was prayer. In his prologue, Benedict conscripts monks as "workmen" whom God is pressing into his service. "The Lord calls out to him and lifts his voice again: *Is there anyone here who yearns for life and desires to see good days?*"[3]

Prayer is central to the life of the Christian. And to pray as Jesus taught his disciples to pray—in Matthew 6 and Luke 11—is to assume a posture foreign to the ethos of most time management advice. Though prayer is certainly an invitation to enter life faithfully, it is not an exercise in our unqualified power to "decide." Prayer is surrender. Prayer is trust. On our knees, we begin by remembering we are not God.

When the crisis cloisters us, I start to pray more. I don't just pray in the early morning hours. I pray as I sit down at my desk to work. I pray at lunch. At dinner, I carry my prayer book to the dining room table to pray with my family, and if I remember to carry it up to my bedroom, I pray on the nights I don't forget and fall asleep. Like Christians of centuries ago, I am trying to practice the habit of praying the daily offices.

I wish I could say this impulse to pray more in early 2020 is an unimpeachably holy one. But it isn't. No, noble intentions do not bring me to my knees in these unprecedented times. I am not like the God-fearing Christians who made fixed-hour prayer—at morning, midday, evening, and bedtime—their daily practice. They wanted to create "a continuous cascade of praise before the throne of God."[4] They considered the hours a hymn: received by God and offered back to him, in thanksgiving and praise.

I, on the other hand, begin praying more because I am anxious. I pray because anxiety has burst from the cage of my chest and seized my arms, and I want to keep it from throbbing at my fingertips. I pray to get relief from the uncertainty of living in a kind of time that can't be measured in the units I'd always depended on.

I pray because I need someplace to hang the towel of a day. I want structure, scaffolding, and order, and if I can't produce something material with my day, at least I can productively pray.

Body Time

When a friend and I took a walk through Allen Gardens after our church reopened, she told me about the new job she'd just landed at a prestigious cosmetics company. "I give all glory to God," she said, with the zeal of a new believer. She was elegant in her wool coat and cashmere scarf, which she tightened in the wind. This friend had more recently come to faith in Christ, and after she joined my small group in the fall of 2020, we began praying for a new job opportunity for her.

"I had nothing to do with manifesting it," my friend added.

"What's 'manifesting'?" I asked.

"You've never heard of manifestation?" she said, a little astonished.

When I Google it later to understand the origins, the first article appears on Oprah Daily. It tells me manifestation has to do with the wildly bestselling book of 2006 called *The Secret*. It involves the phenomenon of "making everything you want to feel and experience a reality . . . via your thoughts, actions, beliefs, and emotions."[5]

Manifestation, in other words, is the very opposite of *receiving* your life from God. It's receiving your life from the universe in the measure that you've "attracted" it to yourself: by focus, by hard work, by intention. According to the article, you can embrace one method of "productive" manifestation popularized on TikTok in which you write down what you want three times in the morning, six times in the afternoon, and nine times at night—for either thirty-three or forty-five days.

I can't help but think how uniquely modern and privileged this impulse is, to "manifest" our lives rather than receive them. A serf in medieval Europe could not have manifested a life beyond the manor and the protection afforded there. A slave in early America could not have manifested a life beyond the plantation and the threat of death. A woman in the early twentieth century could not have manifested the kind of financial independence possible for women today.

Only in our modern technological world can we presume godlike powers for achieving our ends. Surely a hundred years ago, before the invention of antibiotics and insulin and modern vaccines, we held fewer illusions about the realities we could and could not control. It is in no way coincidental that time management, as an industry, grew up in the Industrial Revolution, when machines expanded what humans could accomplish.

Some would say the clock has done more to alter our lives than any other technological invention. Though the mechanical clock was first purposed for keeping regular hours in the monastery, as God's servants moved from cell to chapel, from chapel to field, from field to table, it became a tool for production. The clock gave us time as an objective, external measurement. Eventually, it also gave us categories like "efficiency" and "productivity," pressuring us to think mechanically about our lives.

The clock has given us time as something that marches imperiously forward: one-one thousand, two-one thousand. It has even given us the zeptosecond, one of the smallest units of time that scientists have measured. This is the unit of time for measuring how long it takes a photon to cross a hydrogen molecule: about 247 zeptoseconds.[6] The clock tells "mechanical time," as figured in one chapter of Alan Lightman's bestselling novel, *Einstein's Dreams*. This is time, according to Lightman, that stands in opposition to "body time." One is measured by the clock. The other is measured by heartbeats.

"Each time is time, but the truths are not the same."[7]

In the uniquely embodied experience of a global pandemic, I start to feel how clock time gives way to body time. The days and hours blur, and hurry is burned off my life like morning dew. As anxiety recedes, I start to think about life, about time, as something to receive, not control or manifest by my own productivity measures.

In all the upheaval and uncertainty, this realization is an unexpected gift.

In a lecture entitled "The Tyranny of the Clock and the Gift of Time," Dr. Amber Bowen, professor of philosophy at Redeemer University, tells a group of honors students that she understands how harried they all feel. She begins by calculating, on average, the amount of free time any of them might enjoy in a week. After sixteen to eighteen hours of class time, nine hours of work for each of those classes means fifty-four more hours are spent. Ten more hours are likely dedicated to some extracurricular or community service project, fifteen more hours for paid work. If these students participate in a local church, service organization, or small group, they can lop off another five to seven hours. After eight hours of sleep each night (and an extra hour on the weekend), they're guaranteed a whopping seven full hours of leisure. "It doesn't just feel like there aren't enough hours in the week, there actually aren't enough hours in your week," Dr. Bowen says.[8]

She tells these ambitious, hard-racing students that the week's oversaturation is one reason they experience "time as a threat—as something we must outwit before it outwits us." But all is not lost, she consoles. If we can begin to think of it differently, we'll see that time is "not set *against* us but is a gift *for* us."[9]

A Resistance Movement

On April 13, 2020, I copy this headline in my plague journal: "Limits on Public Life Slow the Outbreak, but Patience Is Wearing Thin." On April 14, I make my first attempt at focaccia: *It's a recipe tried on the most recent episode of* The Great Canadian Baking Show. On April 16, I have a conversation with my neighbor across the street: *He intimated that quarters were tight, that perhaps he and Margaret aren't getting along.*

Within a month, I realize this crisis will not take on the definite boundaries of something begun and suddenly ended. April 22: *I have the sinking feeling that this is our new normal.* On May 20, I make my final record of case counts in Chicago (37,381) and Toronto (8,603). I note that border restrictions between the United States and Canada are set to expire.

Seven months later, Christmas has come and gone, our memory of it recorded on Zoom. Birthdays accumulate. Life grows inward, isolated. When my mother, living in the States, exaggerates the time we've spent apart, I correct her, defending a discrepancy of months. But this is to pretend the difference really matters.

More than a year later, I am no longer writing a plague journal, even if Toronto is battered by a third wave of variant cases and hampered by a lagging vaccine rollout. *August 19: P. and D. came over for wine last night, D. smelling like cologne. They have been matched with a baby boy born several weeks ago.*

In my journal, instead of headlines I copy lines from memorable novels, like Jesmyn Ward's *Sing, Unburied, Sing.* "*I hope I fed you enough. While I'm here. So you can carry it with you. Like a camel. . . . Maybe that ain't a good way of putting it. Like a well, Jojo. Pull that water up when you need it.*"[10] As a family, we enjoy a year's litany of dinner and dusky nights around the firepit. The kids return to school in the fall, and I remember to book tickets for an orchard.

September 20: We started by picking the baking apples: McIntosh and Cortland. We ended by picking the eating apples: Royal Gala and Silken.

The surprise is that gratitude starts to grow wild in my pages.

I start to think that what I'm cataloging is a resistance movement. *A beginning*. I've started to resist the notion that I must earn my keep in this world. Instead, I am receiving the days as a gift. This is, of course, the message of Genesis—and the heartbeat of the gospel. God makes. God gives. This world, ordered as it is by sun and moon, day and night, is our inheritance. God gave us his only Son, in time, that we might have life.

Stand under his sky—and open wide your mouths!

To think of all good things coming from the good hands of God, even time itself, is to see that the hours aren't simply kept. They're *bestowed*. They're *bequeathed*. They're like the goods distributed from another's estate: the bone china, the heirloom wedding ring, the marble-topped table, the moments called *today*. Before we can make something of our lives, even before we can offer them to God, we must be given the raw materials of body and place, even time itself.

We are given our lives, like winter coats for wintry days. This is as staggering and as subversive an assertion as baptism, which is itself a ceremony to figure all we're *receiving* from God: identity, life, blessing, beginning. "God is the actor in baptism, the giver of the gift. . . . Baptism is irrevocable. . . . The initiate freely responds to God receiving baptism."[11] Baptism figures God as benefactor, us as beneficiary; God as giver, us as recipient. Baptism signals that we do not wield the power to manifest reality, only to enter it, at God's bidding, and to receive it, at God's giving.

We don't think today of receiving our identities but of creating them. Invention and reinvention are the modes of contemporary life. Hundreds of years ago, lives were far more confined by geography, by family name, by health and ill health, depending on one's "fortunes." There weren't limitless versions of a life script, each to be authored and pursued by desire. No, a life took shape within constraints.

Even my mother's life choices were more constrained than mine. Born and raised in Akron, Ohio, she went to nursing school there—"Because as a woman, I could either be a nurse, a secretary, or a teacher." She met my father at Akron General Hospital, where he worked as an orderly. He paid for his college tuition (and her engagement ring) by emptying bedpans.

One crisis of time today is that our personal choices seem limitless. We can put on identities like costumes, changing them as the mood suits. Life is ours to construct, to curate, to create. We don't make meaning by mining the world but by manipulating it.[12] And though this may look like freedom, it ends up feeling like imprisonment.

With identity this malleable, we become more and more aspirational. Time becomes more precious and more pressurized, and we end up believing perhaps the ultimate lie: it's all got to count!

Heirs to the Hours

I am speechifying in the car on the how and why of practicing gratitude for all we have received. "Beware of any kind of story you tell about your life that puts you in the center as the hero," I tell my (eye-rolling) children. "You've inherited so many things from others." I imagine this was the lesson Paul was trying to communicate to the Corinthians in one of his many letters. They were a particularly self-congratulating congregation, and Paul rebuked their arrogance: "What do you have that you did not receive? If then you received it, why do you boast as if you did not receive it?"[13]

We are heirs in ways we can hardly appreciate. This is something I learn from Amy Peterson's book *Where Goodness Still Grows*, when she explains the meaning of kindness. We think of kindness as the blandest of virtues. But the word, in its Old English roots, once signaled kinship. As Peterson dug deeper into the history of this word, she discovered that according to the *Oxford English Dictionary*, "*kyndnes* meant 'nation,' or, in legal documents, a right to a title or piece of land based on inheritance."[14] A kindness, in other words, was conferred by social status. It was a measurement of privilege.

"Until recently," Peterson admits,

> I had only rarely considered how the family money I've received has both cushioned and propelled me. . . . The plain truth is that I've had all kinds of advantages, including grandparents who paid for my private school tuition, my summer camp, my music classes, my first car, and some of my first international trips.[15]

Peterson's point isn't just that we should be grateful. No, it's to recognize the structural injustice from which our Black and Indigenous neighbors suffer, who rarely inherit what researcher Joanna Taylor calls a "'transformative asset,' a chunk of money that enables you to pay off student loans, purchase a house, or move to a better neighborhood to send your kids to a better school. For white families that's much more common."[16] To consider kindness in all of these ways is to be forced to doubt the myth of being self-made.

We are receiving our lives, not simply living and making them. I think of W. H. Auden's poem "Horae Canonicae," which follows one person through the canonical hours, or a waking day. At the first hour, *prime*, the speaker of the poem shakes off sleep. This awakening, however, is not an act of agency; it's a summons. The speaker is "recalled from the shades to be a seeing being / From absence to be on display."[17] This first moment of drawing breath is occasion for remembering the nature of worship, that it is an act of grateful response to God for all he's given.

Praise is not productivity. Praise is about the life we receive, arms outstretched, and as we make something of that gift, we recognize it is not anything like God's ex nihilo making. "Gift is a kind of transcendental category," writes theologian John Milbank.

> Creation and grace are gifts; Incarnation is the supreme gift; the Fall, evil and violence are the refusal of gift; atonement is the renewed and hyperbolic gift that is forgiveness; the supreme name of the Holy Spirit is *donum* (according to Augustine); the Church is the community that is given to humanity and is constituted through the harmonious blending of diverse gifts.[18]

A gift is a thing to be received, not demanded and certainly not repaid.

What would happen if we could conceive of the hours in this way?

I think of this question when I remember a recent sermon at church. The preacher is earnest. "If you could just give God five minutes of your day," he says. He wants us to experience the ordinary miracle of walking with Jesus. I am sympathetic to his pleading, and for a moment I am nodding along. I believe spiritual habits, like every other kind of habit, succeed by virtue of modesty. We don't become saints overnight. I believe that five minutes a day—reading the Bible and praying—might be a very good, very necessary place to begin in a newborn life with God. And still, recalling the words of the preacher later, I can't help but find in them something sad, even something embarrassing.

It makes me think of treating God as a pigeon who begs for our scraps. On a recent trip to Chicago, pigeons swarmed us when we carried our lunch to Water Tower Park. The warbling lot circled our feet, hoping for a crumb of a chicken sandwich, a salty French fry. "Don't feed the pigeons!" I told our youngest son, Colin, when he tried to tear his bun and cast its pieces liberally to the hungry crowd.

If we treat God like a pigeon, I wonder about the slack offerings of our five minutes—and shudder to think myself benevolent. It makes me think of the distance we've traveled from previous centuries, arriving at a place when minutes must be cajoled, corralled, coaxed from God's people. When we have lost interest in joining that continuous cascade of praise.

First you learn to count the minutes. Then you learn to find them scarce.

Life, Interrupted

I skip fixed-hour prayer this morning and at lunch. *I'm too busy,* I tell myself. I have thumbed through the remaining pages of the calendar and counted the days I can rely on to meet an important deadline. I've done a little figuring and come up with the impossible number of words I will have to write each one of those days.

Two weeks ago, I sent my children back to school, eager to return to my work after a summer of traveling to see our families and a ten-day graduate school residency. That first Monday morning, on our way to school, my phone rang.

8:04 a.m. It is a friend's husband, who has called to tell me that my friend's mother will die today, that the family put their dog to sleep on Friday, that Saturday was the memorial service for their niece who died earlier that summer at age twenty-six. "It's been a terrible weekend, and I'm thinking we may need to arrange for meals." *Of course!* I say. After I drop off the kids, I don't return to my desk as I've planned but head to the grocery store. Home again, I season chicken thighs and blanch green beans. I cube potatoes and shape dinner rolls—because nothing speaks comfort better than homemade bread.

Two days later, I'm headed out my front door again to take the kids to school then return to my desk. It's a Wednesday, and I'm leaving later than normal.

9:13 a.m. Our contractor, who has built our house and our neighbors' house across the street, gets out of his truck and waves hello. "How are you?" I say, crossing the street to keep from having to shout. I watch him give an ominous shake of the head. "What's wrong?" I ask.

"I have cancer," he says, choking back tears. "Three spots on the lungs. One spot on the liver. It's bad. I need you to pray for me."

"How long are you here?" I ask, nodding toward our neighbors' house, where he's looking after problems with the sump pump. "Let me make you a cup of coffee as soon as I drop the kids at school." If I linger too long, in this moment, they will be late. But how do I tear myself away?

In fifteen minutes, I am pulling back into the driveway. Our contractor is chatting with the neighbors. When Ryan opens our side gate for him, he circles to our backyard. I put a coffee in his hand, and he refuses the seat I offer him, leaning instead over the back of the chair, his trembling hand spilling some of the liquid.

The two of us listen as he talks and begins to cry, then apologizes. "I just want more time. Take an arm. Take a leg. Just give me time with my sons and my grandchildren." Suddenly, the words of the first two verses of John 14 spring into my mind. Jesus is at the cliff of his own death, and it's the disciples who seem to bear all the grief. "Let not your hearts be troubled," he tells them. "Believe in God; believe also in me. In my Father's house are many rooms. If it were not so, would I have told you that I go to prepare a place for you?"

There *is* time, I tell our contractor. Not here, no. Not as much time as we want. But time on the other side, for those united to Jesus by faith. "He's building a house for you," I say, knowing how weird it probably sounds. But he listens, and when I finally get down to the business of praying, long after Ryan has gone inside to take a work call, I promise not to cry. "Oh, God. You tell us that we can pray to you as our Father, and I know my friend knows his own love as a father and grandfather. Can you reassure him that your love for him is infinitely greater than his love for his own family?"

There is no moment of conversion. But it's a time-full moment I receive from the God who orders the minute we leave for school and the minute my contractor arrives, my front door and his truck door opening simultaneously. We could call it serendipity. We could call it providence. We could call it witness to a world held together by God.

Life is set to interruptive mode, it seems. This has been the lesson of the last several weeks, when crises have piled up like smashed cars. After an appointment this morning, I have a frantic text from my diabetic husband, who is at the office. He has been praying and preparing for his first team meeting since March 2020.

> I need help. My pod blew up. Can you bring me another one and more insulin?

He tells me where to find everything.

> Ugh, timing.

I pack up everything he needs and make the forty-five-minute round trip to his office, where his assistant, Sarah, scurries out the front door to take it from me. I'm back home for no more than ten minutes when, this time, I get a frantic call. "Neither of these is working. I need you to get me another one."

This deadline, which is to say *time*, has me hostage. "Can Sarah drive to get them?" I ask.

Who plans to grieve death, get cancer, be subject constantly to the terms of a chronic illness? Who plans on trouble with their teenager and the late-night conversations needed for untangling it? Here's what productivity and efficiency and time management fail to get right. The hours, like our bodies, like the world, aren't under our control. Sure, give me an uninterrupted day (preferably a Monday, after the benefit of Sabbath rest)—and I will charge through a to-do list like a Spanish bull. But don't give me a sick child or an aging parent or a friend in crisis. Don't give me a headache or menstrual cramps. And for goodness' sake, don't give me twins and bored teenagers.

We are receiving our lives—their callings, their constraints. And never has that seemed to allow me to guarantee that I'll even get one thing checked off today's list, no matter how many times I look at the clock. I have, for example, more than two thousand good words of a paper I began writing for an application to a PhD program in 2016. After one abandoned attempt to return to graduate school in 2007, when I learned I was pregnant with twins, I decided I would try again.

I start to get interested in writers whom scholars call the literary domestics, nineteenth-century American women writers who assumed the public role of authorship while also diminishing their own literary efforts. Did their sentimental tales of wives and mothers reinforce the oppressive ideology of separate spheres, as Ann Douglas argued in *The Feminization of American Culture,* or was domesticity itself their means for leveraging cultural power, as promoted by Jane Tompkins in *Sensational Designs*? I engage this question for several furious weeks, as I round up recommendations from professors in undergraduate and graduate school who I hope will remember me.

And then I stop. Careen to a halt. This is to say, before the application deadline, I give up. I meet the end of this ambition, despite Ryan's encouragement. "You can do it!" he says. But I can't. And I know I can't. Not with the other things I have come to value—and have *received*—from God. My children. My third contracted book. My local church.

Have I failed to make a life? Or am I learning to receive one?

"It is hard for you to kick against the goads."[19] This one-liner, delivered by Jesus to Saul on the road to Damascus, is like an echo in my head. It seems to say something about our resistance to receiving the life God chooses to give us. I confess that I don't really know what goads are, even if I know myself to be kicking against them. Like everyone else, I can find myself wishing I had a life other than my own. I wish I had a sibling, a cousin, a graying, balding father. I wish I had no responsibilities for an aging mother, no responsibilities for school pickup and drop-off. I wish someone else would make dinner tonight.

I am good at this kind of complaining. It's also true that in the first moments of the morning, when the house is swaddled in quiet, I try practicing another habit—the habit of receiving life with gratitude. I wake, as poet W. H. Auden puts it, "between my body and the day"[20] and thank God for the feel of the sheets, for the breathing form of my husband lying beside me. I name thanks for many things, then recite the prayer I've learned to pray in important moments of surprise, whenever life has headed somewhere unexpected. I surrender to the marvel, the miracle, the mystery of this moment called *now* and reach to receive it. "Whatever you choose to give, Lord, I embrace."

TO CONSIDER

What seasons, what interruptions have been hardest for you to receive?

What would be different if you looked to receive your life from God, not simply manage or change it?

What new freedom can you enjoy, knowing time is a gift?

TO PRAY

God, you are the one who wakes me into the mercies of each new day. My body and breath are gifts from you, and I often fail to give thanks for them. Please forgive me this ingratitude. Thank you for the gift of time and the gift of its responsibilities. Before I seek to manage the hours, before I seek to make something of my life, teach me to receive all you give as a kindness from your hands.

Belong

As we commit ourselves to relationships, we lose time—
and find life as God intended it.

I start sending journal prompts to my mother in the
early weeks of April 2020. "Write about your parents,"
I suggest. "What were their dates of birth, marriage, and
death? Where and how did they meet? Tell a story about
each of them that captures how you remember them from
your childhood."

I am sending these questions, in part, to keep her busy.
She and my stepfather are shut up in their assisted living facility without visitors or any opportunity to leave.
Sheared like a branch after a storm, they are now severed
from the people they care most about: our family of seven,
now stuck across an international border; my stepsister
and her husband, who take to waving at them from the
parking lot; their church family, whom they now only see
over Zoom.

Initially, my mother is excited about this family history project. She starts to send back answers to my prompts. Her responses, however, are mostly scant, with occasional exceptions. "My favorite teacher in elementary school was Miss Hansen in the fifth grade. That year, my friend Cynthia was chosen to sing in a huge concert at the Armory in downtown Akron. She was sick, so I got to go." But after several weeks, my mom stops sending answers, and I stop sending prompts.

As the weeks drag on, I also try remembering my responsibilities to my dad's sister, Ruthie, who lives alone in Indiana. She, too, lives in a congregate setting: a government subsidized apartment building at the edge of town.

Conversations with my aunt have long tended toward a rehearsal of the same details. Because she is dying of kidney failure, she is putting money away for the headstone. *"Honey, I don't want you to be responsible for that."* She tells me, many times over, that the cedar chest is intended for a friend in town. *"Do the girls want the china?"* She wishes that her belongings, at least those I don't come to claim *"Within a couple of weeks, honey,"* be donated to Resale to the Rescue, whose profits support local animal welfare organizations. Ruthie has an old cat, which I hope doesn't outlive her.

My mother and my aunt make the list of people I want to check in on during the hardship of this time. That list also includes friends who work in health care and friends who aren't married. This is to say not all my pandemic lists are as self-interested as productivity lists (many of my own included) can tend to be.

In her book *Counterproductive,* Melissa Gregg notes the self-fulfilling nature of the tasks Edwin Bliss proposes for a theoretical "someday list" in his 1976 book also named *Getting Things Done*:

> that special course you want to take to upgrade your professional skills; that new project you would like to suggest to your boss after you find time to do the preliminary fact-finding; that article you've been meaning to write; that diet you've intended to begin; that annual medical check you've planned to get for the last three years; that visit to your lawyer to have your will drawn; that retirement program you've been planning to establish.[1]

There is an individualist ethic in time management, Gregg notes. *You* are working to achieve *your* best life now.

The premise of time management is control, and one way to achieve control is to eliminate contingency. Contingency is, of course, a feature of social human life. To belong to one another is to suffer the loss of independence, the loss of protected, cherished time.

Women know this truth well. I remember my blood simmering to a boil years ago while listening to an interview with Daniel Pink, author of *When: The Scientific Secrets of Perfect Timing.* Drawing from research in the fields of psychology, biology, and economics, Pink concluded there were empirically better times of the day for certain activities. I wondered what a morning without the contingencies of family breakfast and missing uniforms and school car pool might be like. Yes, I could be well on my way to writing the next great American novel.

I've certainly been guilty of the self-dependent bent in time management as well. But this, too, began to shift during the pandemic with its vocabulary of *public* health and *collective* action and *herd* immunity. As we were separated from one another and restricted from gathering, it started to become important to recover a sense of corporate identity, figured in the images of the Bible: a family, a house, a temple, a body, a vine of many branches. It started to become impossible to see myself as anything other than a member among many wider communities: a family, a neighborhood, a city, a nation.

To think of immunity, writes Eula Biss, is to consider how the boundaries between bodies dissolve. Self and other are not as separate as we might once have thought.[2]

Life, Interrupted Again

"I heard you're thinking of moving," my neighbor says to me when I show up at her door to borrow a portable jump starter for our car, which is now dead in the driveway. "My mother isn't well," I begin. She nods, and I remember that she has been caring for her aging mother since her father died a year earlier. I don't tell her that the discussion of moving has resuscitated old resentments with Ryan, that we're having lots of conversations beginning with some version of "It's hard to be a woman."

Instead I tell her how, on our first visit back to the States in the summer of 2021, more than eighteen months since I'd last seen my mother, ordinary plans required multiple rehearsals. I tell her I caught my mother looking blank in the middle of conversations, nodding along as if she understood. I describe how, after the visit, I started making worried phone calls. I called the director at the assisted living facility. I called their insurance agent. I talked to the financial planner and started asking for copies of important documents, which my mother dutifully carried down to the office manager to scan and email to me.

"Honor your father and mother, right?" I add, standing on my neighbor's driveway. She is leaning in the doorway with her dog in her arms. "Isn't that a core tenet of our faiths?" My Jewish neighbor nods. Truthfully, I feel a bit sheepish for how obvious this is supposed to be—and how difficult I find it at the very same time. I never really want the interruptions that belonging visits upon my life, these "claims" and "tyrannies," as Virginia Woolf calls them in *A Room of One's Own*.

After we returned from our summer visit to the States, I began running headlong into several proverbs reminding me of my responsibilities as a daughter to my mother. "Don't despise your mother when she is old!" "May she who gave you birth be happy!" "What a pleasure to have children who are wise!"

"God does not move us like stones," I read in a prayer book. *But maybe,* I think, sitting in my chair with a view of the street, *he rains them from the sky to provide motivation.*

"Sometimes it's just so hard to be a woman," I say to Ryan, as we stand in front of the bathroom mirror getting ready for church. "There are so many people to take care of, and the responsibility is always falling on our shoulders."

I am applying eyeliner—and thinking of the past twenty-five years of marriage. It doesn't help I am reading *A Room of One's Own* for my MFA and have just happened upon the part when Woolf imagines Shakespeare's fictional sister.

> She was as adventurous, as imaginative, as agog to see the world as he was. But she was not sent to school. She had no chance of learning grammar and logic, let alone of reading Horace and Virgil. She picked up a book now and then, one of her brother's perhaps, and read a few pages. But then her parents came in and told her to mend the stockings or mind the stew and not moon about books and papers.[3]

I prattle on—and I am angry when, midsentence, I notice Ryan has set down his toothbrush and turned to leave. I resent even this prerogative of his: to ignore the conversation.

But Ryan is not to blame. Closer to the truth is that neither of us is good at belonging, at this habit that assumes interdependence and need. "Does this have something to do with early trauma?" the marriage counselor asks us after that morning conversation in the bathroom.

"So you both lost your fathers when you were young?" she continues. Yes, Ryan was three months from high school graduation when his father, ill with a rare pulmonary disease, died unexpectedly at Rush University Hospital in Chicago. Yes, I was two months from my nineteenth birthday when I took the phone call from my mother at the dining hall at Wheaton College: "Your father's dead. You need to come home."

Am I speaking for the both of us? I wonder.

When you live long enough with self-reliance, you don't quite know how to shake it. It is a sticky and stubborn habit. In our serial transience as a family, moving to follow my father for his graduate work then various faculty positions, we established ourselves as a "pioneer tree species"—like quaking aspen, silver birch, and pussy willow. We were characterized by distance traveled. In my mind's eye, I am in the third seat of our boxy, beige Pontiac station wagon, and we are somewhere between Indiana and Missouri, Missouri and Tennessee, Tennessee and Ohio. It is summer or Christmas vacation, and I am looking out the car window. Tall lone oaks blur past, and I imagine the solitary hours I will spend in their shade, burrowed in a book.

In my recent fascination with trees, I've learned about the difference between American redwoods and European redwoods. According to German forester Peter Wohlleben, European redwoods have often been planted "in city parks by princes and politicians as exotic trophies," and don't achieve the growth of their American counterparts.[4] Unlike American redwoods, which populate undisturbed forests, European redwoods grow up without aunts and uncles, cousins, or even parents. Raised in nurseries, they have root balls kept small by deliberate trimming to make the trees easier to move.

Unfortunately, this root damage is trauma from which the European redwoods never recover. They don't develop the extended root and fungal networks that would allow them to share resources with other trees. Many are fated to root themselves shallowly, perpetually vulnerable to storm. They are top-heavy trees with an enormous crown—and only twenty inches of below-the-soil support.

In Germany, city oaks, like the urban redwoods, also suffer a solitary fate. A moth called the oak processionary loves to feed on their

> warm crowns, drenched in sunlight. In the middle of the forest, these [pests] are hard to find. The few oaks that grow in the forest are mixed in with beeches, and only their topmost tips reach the light. In the city, however, oaks stand out in the open, where they are warmed by the sun all day long.[5]

Isolation, then, is the quality that makes for a feast. "The caterpillars love this."[6]

Proverbs 31 Productivity

"What is the one image in the Bible that figures the healthy human life, the life that thrives in God?" I scan the room in a Toronto church basement, waiting for one of these college students to answer my question. This is one of my first speaking events since COVID canceled most of my calendar. I pause and wait, then finally say, "Turn to Psalm 1."

"A tree!" someone in the front row exclaims.

"Yes, a tree." We open this psalm, which many scholars have called a "wisdom" psalm, and consider together the deeply rooted, regularly watered human life.

> Blessed is the man
> who walks not in the counsel of the wicked . . .
> but his delight is in the law of the LORD,
> and on his law he meditates day and night.

> He is like a tree
>> planted by streams of water
> that yields its fruit in its season,
>> and its leaf does not wither.[7]

This psalm is conveying an important truth, and it is not structured as an alliterated three-point sermon.

It's a vision of canopies and roots—a poetic picture of health.

I explain that editors placed it here, along with Psalm 2, as an introduction to this book of prayers. And what is prayer, I ask, if not the language of familial belonging? I note that these pray-ers feel as if they have some right to make claims on God: "Give ear to my words, O LORD; consider my groaning. Hear a just cause, O LORD, attend to my cry! But you, O LORD, do not be far off!"[8] This is at the heart of prayer's mystery, of course. That the God from whom we are receiving our lives would seem to make himself subject to our requests, even what sound like our demands.

It is an October day, and Toronto's canopy is burnishing red and yellow and orange. I tell this group of students that the tree of Psalm 1 is a tree planted by God, planted where the conditions are right for growth. This is a tree that enjoys stability, a tree that is not victim to wind or storm or drought. According to the Tanakh translation of the Hebrew Bible, this is a tree that is "planted beside streams of water, which yields its fruit in season, whose foliage never fades, and whatever it produces thrives."[9]

I get stuck, of course, on that word *produces* in my preparation for this talk. I learn, from *The Jewish Study Bible*, that this productivity does not look like the Pomodoro technique or Inbox Zero, that it has nothing to do with time maps and tickler files. No, this is productivity that looks like belonging, with the supposed inefficiencies of family life. "Living to a ripe old age and having many children is the biblical idea for a successful life."[10]

It sets me thinking back to the spring of 2007, when I showed up to the campus of Wheaton College and climbed the stairs to the department of modern and classical languages. Audrey had just finished kindergarten. Nathan would start the following year, and Camille would begin preschool the year after. I could glimpse a future beyond the intensity of caring for three young children, and I imagined starting Wheaton's biblical exegesis program with my newfound time.

Less than a month later, I learned I was pregnant. Another month later, I learned I was pregnant with twins.

For far too long, I narrowly imagined one version of productivity in my life—and it was not the productivity of Psalm 1. I had little appreciation for the interdependence at the heart of flourishing family and forest life. I could see only cost, not profit. But trees, I've learned, benefit from life in a neighborhood. They "exchange news about insects, drought and other dangers."[11] They share sugars as if they are portable jump starters for cars dead in driveways. Because gaps in the canopy can cause trees to suffer damage from drought or storms, every tree "is valuable to the community and worth keeping around as long as possible."[12] To be a tree, sheltered in the wide canopy of community, isn't to be unbothered but to be safe.

In this way, trees don't practice the logic of "efficiency." They don't reserve resources for the highest producers. They tend to their weaker members, as the body of Christ is commanded to do. "If one member suffers, all suffer together; if one member is honored, all rejoice together."[13] Trees look to strengthen all members of the family, even the ailing aunts and aging mothers. When trees grow together, they create an ecosystem that moderates extreme temperatures, stores water, and controls humidity. In this protected environment, "trees can live to be very old."[14] When we reimagine God's call to forest life, we will recover the value of caring for the most vulnerable among us: the young, the old, the sick, the differently abled.

To be clear, I am not suggesting that belonging is a feature exclusive to a biological family. As a Christian, *family* becomes a far more relative term. "Who is my mother, and who are my brothers?" Jesus once asked the crowd.[15]

Everyone gets to belong in the kingdom of God, whether or not you drive a minivan. Because God looks after the belonging of his people. "Father of the fatherless and protector of widows is God in his holy habitation. God settles the solitary in a home."[16] Married or unmarried, childless or child-full, we are all invited into the benefits and burdens of belonging.

I talked to my mother twice on the phone last weekend. On Saturday, she's excited to tell me about the one-year anniversary party their assisted-living facility is throwing that afternoon. "They didn't tell us we could've invited friends, or I would have invited Marianne." On Sunday afternoon, she's excited to tell me about the brick oven pizza they served at the party and the "world's most delicious brownies." "They didn't tell us we could have invited friends, or I would have invited Marianne." She doesn't realize she has repeated herself.

And I don't tell her. Instead, I pray for a growing capacity to grow sheltering limbs of love.

Resistance to Love's Demands

In the introduction to *I Know How She Does It*, Laura Vanderkam describes a visit to a local pick-your-own strawberry farm, where she finds a time management lesson hidden among the baskets. "Remember the berry season is short. This box holds approximately 10 lbs level full, 15 lbs heaping full."[17] Vanderkam is a proponent of the time map, and I open my own time map from June 2020: a month represented in little squares of thirty minutes. This time, I try noticing not just the *projects* but the *people*.

On Monday, at 10:00 a.m., I call my nephew James. On Tuesday, at noon, I walk with the twins around the block. On Wednesday, I leave at 1:30 to take groceries to my friend Constance. On Thursday, we ride our bikes as a family at 5:00. On Friday, at 1:30, I call my mom. I don't record what happens on Friday and Saturday, but I do know I've promised a proposal for another project, and it's still not finished.

Pandemic belonging has proven to be a source of interruption for my professional work. For more than a year, my husband was battered by the unrelenting demands of work and elder responsibilities at our church. There was slack to pick up in his bleary-eyed exhaustion, even mild depression. My oldest was home from college, and my other four children were finishing the school year online. They were self-sufficient mostly, but they still needed to be fed. My immigrant friend was shut inside with her three little boys and without a way to get groceries, and I was suddenly struck by the insight that the apostle James called true religion: the act of *visiting* the widow and the orphan.[18]

When I finally turned something in to my editor, an entire year later than promised, it was a proposal I hammered out at my dining room table as the family orbited around me like Jupiter's many moons. "I can have it finished by the end of the year," I reassured her.

This was a promise I made—and failed to keep. Because I decided to visit my friend Heather in Scotland after her metastatic breast cancer diagnosis. Because we drove to visit a potential school for our twins as we planned for the possibility of moving. Belonging did not give way to my deadlines, even if I decided against seeing Janet, who was passing her last days in one of Toronto's city-run long-term care facilities. Before church shuttered, she had sat alone in an adjacent pew at church, scribbling sermon notes into her spiral notebook. I wanted to go, and I decided I couldn't because deadlines loomed.

I think of Vanderkam's optimism about time and her metaphor of the moving tiles, that creativity will make everything possible. I don't believe her. Because something always gives, doesn't it? And the agonizing question is always, *What?*

When I revisited the Proverbs 31 woman recently, so often hailed as the paragon of time management, I wasn't as impressed by the chores and obligations she was ticking from her lists. Instead, I began noticing the communities to which she belongs. The heart of her husband trusts in her. Her children rise up and call her blessed. She provides food for her household and portions for her maidens. She opens her hands to the poor and reaches out to the needy. This is not a hymn to the woman who gets things done but a celebration of the woman who, fearing the Lord, makes herself vulnerable to the needs of others.

A fruitful life, according to Proverbs 31 and Psalm 1—and really, the whole story of the Bible—is a life of belonging and connection, contingency and love. *It is not good for man to be alone,* God himself noted when Adam struck a solitary figure in the garden. And though most of us assume we want a life of belonging, we're also deeply afraid of its costs. As the December 2018 cover story for the *Atlantic* explored, young people today have fewer romantic relationships than their parents and grandparents did. They're even having less sex, preferring, as some sociologists speculate, the autonomous pleasures of masturbation to the complicated joys of commitment.[19]

Acedia, I learn, is one word to use in talking about our resistance to the habit of belonging. Acedia has held various places on the lists of the seven (or eight) deadly sins, and it's not a word many of us are familiar with today. Although acedia is a way to speak about the sin of sloth, it's far too easy—and too dangerous—to assume acedia always keeps us on the couch, rewatching episodes of *The Office.*

Evagrius, in the fourth century—and later John Cassian, Pope Gregory I, and Aquinas—wrote about the two faces of acedia. On the one hand, acedia can look like physical listlessness—or pandemic "languishing," as psychologist

Adam Grant termed it in the most-read *New York Times* article of 2021. It can look like despondency, like depression, and it can draw you away from the relationships you've previously valued. "You don't catch yourself slipping slowly into solitude; you're indifferent to your indifference. When you can't see your own suffering, you don't seek help or even do much to help yourself."[20]

But acedia's antisocial nature doesn't only manifest behind drawn shades in the blinking, blue light of the TV. What the monks understood, quite helpfully, was that acedia could also look like busyness. It could look like reorganizing the pantry and sorting through a backlog of old pictures. Acedia could be frantically productive—so long as its attentions remained misdirected, its devotions misaimed. Whether it was sluggish or hyperactive, the monks understood that acedia always had to do with *escape*. We don't want to commit ourselves to the painful efforts required for our transformation. We don't want to participate in the work of loving God or loving our neighbor well.

As Rebecca Konyndyk DeYoung puts it, acedia is "resistance to love's demands."[21] Only God himself can cure the disease of our self-chosen loneliness.

A Threefold Cord

Perhaps there is nothing like forced isolation to make us cherish what the New Testament writers call *koinonia,* or fellowship. This word signals what we share *in common*. It reminds us of the gift of *communion*. Our church closed its doors on March 15, 2020, and didn't reopen them until June 20, 2021.

I wrote about that reopening in my "Letter from the Editor" for *Imprint*:

> I choked back a small sob on the Sunday of my return to 383 Jarvis, on June 20, 2021. It was the singing that did it. To hear the chorus of Christ's body singing in unison, after so many months of pandemic silence, was to believe we'd survived a long, Narnian winter.[22]

Winter might be the best way to describe my COVID experience: that it has been a dropping of leaves and a conserving of energy. A languishing, a listlessness, and also a preparation for something new. I haven't gotten the things I've wanted to do done, true. But I've deepened my sense of belonging to others. Maybe even I've begun healing some resentments.

"The dropping of leaves by deciduous trees is called abscission," Katherine May writes in *Wintering*. As the days grow shorter and the temperature falls, she explains, it becomes too costly for trees to maintain growth. "A layer of cells is weakening between the stem and the branch: this is called the abscission zone."[23]

I think of how the red leaves will fall from my Japanese maple outside my front door, how in January it will look skeletal, frail, dead. But as May explains in her book, a wintering tree is a tree in bud. It produced its buds in high summer—and now the tree is waiting. "It is far from dead. It is in fact the life and soul of the wood. It's just getting on with it quietly. It will not burst into life in the spring. It will just put on a new coat and face the world again."[24] When those first leaves fall, it only takes hours for the tree to heal the scar those leaves have left behind, those open sores vulnerable to infection and parasites.

It is shocking to think of the pandemic, which has visited so much disaster on the world, as a measure of health. But this has been its severe mercy, that it has restored to some of us the sense that we must care for one another during real hardships.

As pandemic restrictions began easing, I faced the world again and the people in it. I considered anew what responsibilities I owed to others, what necessary burdens those responsibilities would entail. I offered to lead a small group. I hosted dinners again. I made time to talk to my elderly neighbor, Gail, across the street. We started marriage counseling. I called my mother. I called my children. None of this was efficient work. It took time and patience. People are not projects.

Given the ever-present temptation of acedia, this craving to have the good life with the least effort possible, I understand my interest in belonging will be subject to constant threat. To be sure, I think it will have to be watered. The pandemic has reminded us of the costs of belonging, even our unwillingness to sacrifice ourselves for others. I think Tish Harrison Warren put it well in her opinion piece for the *New York Times*. While some wanted a quick return to "normal," especially parents for their children, she says there are important lessons in the crisis not to be quickly overlooked.

"The failure to learn empathy and civic duty," Warren writes,

> is a fate worse than having to forgo birthday parties, graduations, and play dates. The problem with parents

117

focusing on how to "get out" of Covid precautions . . . is that it teaches privileged kids that the problems of the world aren't their responsibility.[25]

Maybe this is belonging, at its heart. Not just membership but a sense of shared responsibility. I am your keeper, and you are mine.

The Teacher, as he's called in the book of Ecclesiastes, searches out the meaning of our brief days and looks to draw conclusions on what makes life worth living. Not wine, not wealth, not great works, he concludes.

> I built houses and planted vineyards for myself. I made gardens and parks and planted in them all kinds of fruit trees. I made myself pools with which to water the forest of growing trees. . . . I became great and surpassed all who were before me in Jerusalem. . . . Then I considered all that my hands had done and the toil I had expended in doing it, and behold, all was vanity and a striving after wind, and there was nothing to be gained under the sun.[26]

Here was a man who got things done—and found himself miserable. What advice, then, does this Teacher have to give?

Belong, he writes. Belong to God, fearing him and keeping his commandments. "This is the whole duty of man."[27] Belong, too, to others:

> Two are better than one, because they have a good reward for their toil. For if they fall, one will lift up his fellow. But woe to him who is alone when he falls and has not another to lift him up! Again, if two lie together, they keep warm,

but how can one keep warm alone? And though a man might prevail against one who is alone, two will withstand him—a threefold cord is not quickly broken.[28]

At first glance, the only "reward" I can see for the combined toil of these two people is greater productivity. They arrive at the mall, like my mother and I, and part ways. They *divide and conquer*. But no, this is not what the Teacher has in mind at all. He is accounting for the suffering of life and the comfort we draw from the company of others. He is seeing trees in the protected ecosystem of a crowded forest.

"It sounds like you're hoping to heal some past wounds and practice greater attachment," the marriage therapist says in our one-on-one session. "And that makes sense to me, as you feel the pressures of caring for your mother. You want someone to turn to, to rely on, to understand your inner world." I nod, thinking of Katherine May's description of the abscission zone.

Ryan and I have decided that there is no one person to blame for the individualistic—and in one sense, heartily productive—system of our marriage. The one that has produced five children. The one that has put him through eight years of actuarial exams, then an MBA. The one I rely on now to meet my deadlines, while Ryan picks up the boys from basketball practice. The one that has *divided and conquered*.

We're at a beginning, even in this middle of our lives. We will learn to belong to each other in more meaningfully intimate ways. We will learn to offer that belonging to our own children, even to our own parents. We will even consider the trauma of an uprooting in another cross-border move, if God sees fit.

The story of salvation travels from tree to tree to tree. The first trees of the garden set up the stark polarity that runs through the pages of the Bible, even the vision of Psalm 1. There are only two ways in life: the way of wisdom and the way of foolishness; the way of blessing and the way of cursedness; the way of the righteous and the way of the wicked. The tree of the cross reminds us how we mistake one for the other. "When Jesus calls a man, he bids him come and die."[29]

Together, Ryan and I will learn, in the days that remain, to receive this life with all its responsibilities, all its important and urgent demands of love. We will try to make belonging our habit. "Those with acedia . . . cannot fully accept the only thing that would ultimately bring them joy. They refuse the thing they most desire, and they turn away from the only thing that can bring them life."[30] This will be a long learning, and it will require a lifetime of practice.

But trees, I read, have the luxury of time.

TO CONSIDER

What prevents you from vulnerably practicing the habit of belonging?

What habits of self-focus and self-dependence have proven to serve you unreliably?

What relationships do you most value, and what further investment can you make to strengthen and deepen them?

TO PRAY

God, you are a community of persons, Father, Son, and Holy Spirit. Thank you for drawing me into your own circle of belonging and bearing the costs of love's demands on the cross. Help me to surrender my habits of self-reliance, my long histories of resentment, and my subtle resistance to belonging as I am formed into the image of your Son, Jesus Christ, and joined to his church.

Offer

As we inhabit time faithfully, we discover that worship, not usefulness, is the greatest gift we offer.

The first time I meet David and Beth Booram, I find them on the spacious covered porch of their hundred-year-old home. It is 2015. David's long gray hair is pulled back in a ponytail. Beth's graying hair falls neatly in a smooth bob. It's a July evening, and the cicadas are humming in this urban Indianapolis neighborhood.

I've left my children at my mother's house in Columbus, three hours away, and have planned to spend a week at the Boorams' home. Since 2012, they've offered their four guest bedrooms—two on the second floor, two on the third—as retreat space, which they've named Fall Creek Abbey. This week, I have a book to finish at the Abbey—or, as I later learn, a book to pull apart and start piecing back together. I'll do that work on a small table underneath an eave, overlooking the street.

Before opening the Abbey, David and Beth spent their lives in church and parachurch work. I only know scant details of what led to their resignation and the intervening years of trying to figure out what was next, some of which are discussed in Beth's book *Starting Something New*. But I do know that by the time I first arrive at their doorstep and their blue-and-brown-eyed dog, Bongo, follows me upstairs, I feel as if I've been received as Christ himself. At Fall Creek Abbey, I come to learn what it means to receive the offering of another's unhurried presence—which I drink down like a cup of cold water.

Until travel becomes far more difficult in 2020, I make routine visits to the Abbey. I come to write, to rest, and also to learn from Beth and David as we sit for many hours around the table that affords a view of the backyard and the bird feeders. For all the years I've known them, I've admired the time-full living the Boorams have engaged in their new vocation, one that involves loads of laundry and multiple trips to Costco—though, at least in my observation, very little panic. Beth likes to remind me this requires, among other disciplines, "the spiritual practice of calendaring."

Vocation is a word for talking about the way we offer our lives—our time—to God in worship. *Vocation* underscores the reality of higher time: if the days are a gift, then life is a calling. "You are not your own, for you were bought with a price. So glorify God in your body."[1] Vocation captures what it means to daily respond to the Christ who offered himself on our behalf. *Here am I*, he said.

To the call of the self-giving Christ, vocation answers: here I am, O God. Everything I am and have belongs to you.

I've often heard Beth and David talk about their understanding of hospitality as vocation. This calling, they've explained, is not the stage-lit spectacle that substitutes for ministry in many public spaces these days. It is a quiet, unassuming, *listening* vocation. Importantly, its orientation is first inward and upward—a practice of the ears before a habit of the hands.

In the Boorams' case, the obedient practice of vocation begins with silent hours before breakfast, behind closed office doors. Every morning I've creaked down the stairs to their kitchen to pour my first cup of freshly ground coffee, I've imagined that to open either of those doors would be to find David and Beth as radiant-faced as Moses. I've imagined them on their knees, praying for the humility vocation requires. *Your projects, your purposes today, Lord. Your fame and your glory.*

It reminds me of the opening scene of *A Burning in My Bones*, the biography of one of my favorite writers, the late Eugene Peterson. Author Winn Collier opens the narrative with Eugene's wife sending their young son to fetch his father for breakfast. It's a few minutes after 7:00 a.m. "Eric, go tell Dad breakfast is ready." Eric was nine years old, and he tiptoed down the stairs to his father's basement office. He found Eugene on his knees, wrapped in a prayer shawl, a Hebrew psalter open in front of him, rocking gently. "Eric watched, hushed. He slowly closed the door and crept back upstairs, to the clink of forks against plates. Only a boy, but he knew he'd witnessed something holy."[2]

Time management experts, of course, extol the benefits of rising early. Just yesterday, I read an article about "The Quiet Joys of the Very, Very Early Morning Club."[3]

The author enumerates the benefits of 4:00 a.m., when the rest of the world—including his young children—are sleeping. And while I, too, can be a publicist for predawn, that isn't my purpose here. If there is any secret magic to 4:00 a.m., it is the quiet of the house, the world, the head.

To speak of vocation, what counts isn't productivity (or, God forbid, *impact*).[4] What counts is knowing that time belongs not to us but to God. What counts is the act of offering ourselves to God, over and over and over again: "Morning by morning he awakens; he awakens my ear to hear as those who are taught. The Lord GOD has opened my ear, and I was not rebellious."[5] What counts in vocation are habits of consecration, made in response to divine grace.

Here I am, here I am, here I am. How many saints have started here, voicing these three simple words of faith? Abraham on Mount Moriah. Jacob in his feverish night dreams. Moses in the wilderness. Samuel as a young boy. Isaiah in a vision. Only Mary, soon-to-be mother of God, changed the script slightly when Gabriel thudded into her mother's kitchen in the middle of the week: "Behold, I am a servant of the Lord: let it be to me according to your word."[6]

It seems to me that consecration involves contemplation, by which I mean to include the regular intake of God's words. Vocation arises out of blinding encounter with the living God. In Robert Alter's translation and commentary, I learn more about the meaning of the Hebrew verb *hagah* of Psalm 1:1–2, which is translated "studies" in the Tanakh, "meditates" in the ESV, and "murmurs" by Alter: "Happy the man who has not walked in the wicked's counsel, nor in the way of offenders has stood, nor in the session of scoffers has sat. But the LORD's teaching is his desire, and His teaching he *murmurs* day and night."[7]

Hagah, Alter writes, means to "make a low muttering sound."[8] He reminds readers that ancient cultures did not practice silent reading. Meditation was, for ancient Jews, as much a habit of the mouth as the mind.[9] It was an active process, not a rote spiritual exercise. I wonder if *hagah* suggests that behind the closed doors of David's and Beth's offices, behind the door Eric Peterson pushed open at age nine, it's not as quiet as we imagine.

I'm muttering too, when I rock in the Poang Ikea chair in my third-floor bedroom of Fall Creek Abbey, my Bible splayed open on my lap.

Eugene Peterson was as taken as I am with the verb *hagah*. In the early pages of *Eat This Book*, he notes it is the same verb used in Isaiah 31:4, where the translation reads "a young lion *growls* over his prey." *Hagah*, Peterson explains, "is a word that our Hebrew ancestors used frequently for reading the kind of writing that deals with our souls."[10]

"I am interested," Peterson continues, "in cultivating this kind of reading, the only kind of reading that is congruent with what is written in our Holy Scriptures, but also with all writing that is intended to change our lives and not just stuff some information into the cells of our brain."[11] Peterson is talking about a habit of reading the Bible that involves transformation, not simply information. A reading that makes it possible for us to offer our lives in service, in ministry—or, as the Hebrew word *avodah* suggests, in work and worship.

I like to think Peterson is imagining meditative moments when God's people draw up water from deep invisible reservoirs. Moments of invitation—God's people learning to live in response to his voice. Human lives formed by this habit may not *impact* the world—a word denoting "concentrated force over a short amount of time."[12] Instead, they will bear fruit like trees.[13]

I recently learned that vocation has, at its root, words like *call* and *summons*, *cleric* and *ecclesiastical*. Vocation is like a two-step dance. In some pocket of the day's quiet, we're called out of the world. Then, ever so suddenly, we are summoned back to it.[14]

First Order of Business? *Rest*

The first time I meet her, my long-billed friend is standing haughtily on a pair of my son's swim trunks slung over the half wall of the porch. I am praying, and the sun is just starting to peek over the trees. It is the first pandemic summer, and we are, in Canadian parlance, "cottaging."

The second time I meet my hummingbird, she is in flight. Again, I am praying. I am startled by a loud buzzing noise. My eyes jerk open to see my friend hovering inches from my nose, her wings beating so fast as to make the movement imperceptible. She hangs in midair for several seconds, then darts away. This happens again, several days later. Each visit I receive as an annunciation.

Consider the birds, Jesus said, though I'd never taken him seriously.

In these early morning hours on the porch of this century-old cottage, I am also reading a book called *When*

Poets Pray by Marilyn McEntyre. McEntyre remembers her own mother's pleasure at watching the hummingbirds feed outside the kitchen window of her childhood home. She would call Marilyn over to witness the birds hovering at the feeder, drinking the sweet syrup of dinner. "The stillness of the hummingbird in midair offers its own particular fascination. What is it waiting for? Thinking? Or doing just there before it dives into the next flower or flies off to its nesting place?"[15]

These are some of the indulgences of this vacation: considering the birds, reading poetry, swimming, even spending a long afternoon inside the dock house watching a storm roll in. The owners of the cottage are Christians, and in the packet of instructions they've sent us for the week, they've included a short Scripture verse to express their hopes for our time in their home: "And Jesus said to them, 'Come away by yourselves to a desolate place and rest a while' (Mark 6:31)."

We've done this. *Come away*. During this week by the lake, we are not getting things done. We are sitting still. Sitting still is not what productive people do, of course, and it's not usually our habit. Productive people whir like machines. They glow with blue light. But as I come to learn, this sitting still is essential to vocation.

According to the Bible, vocation begins with rest.

Rest was the indulgent gift offered by God to Adam and Eve at the curtain opening of the world. After all the flurry of activity, after the cosmic charge to make something of the world he had made, God let his people loose into the luxuriant hours of Sabbath. God himself rested—and made space, in his own rest, for welcome. The first task for keeping God's hours was not to make a difference in the world. Instead, it was to enter God's rest, the rest made possible because of the work God had already done.

The Sabbath is a day to remember that whatever we make, whatever we produce, whatever we offer of our lives and our time, it will not keep the world spinning on its axis. That's God's job. As A. J. Swoboda puts it in *Subversive Sabbath,*

> The picture is stunning—the first day for Adam and Eve was not a day to work the garden. God established a weekly rhythmic reminder of his love—the Sabbath. Again, the Bible offers a view of God that is so entirely unlike the gods of other religions' creation narratives. No other god gives rest.[16]

Rest is a gift, offered to us by God before we ever attempt to offer anything back to him. In economies of production, of course, rest may be one of the hardest gifts to receive from God. We want to produce to prove our usefulness, our worth. We want to run to make God proud.

John Cassian writes about the temptations of "usefulness" in his fifth-century *Institutes,* as he describes the monk beset by the deadly sin of acedia, or sloth. The monk's "dejection," he notes, sets in just about noon when the sun is hanging highest over his head. He has already been at the work of prayer or study for several hours, and he has grown tired of the efforts required for this work that makes no visible, measurable progress.

> He often groans because he can do no good while he stays there, and complains and sighs because he can bear no spiritual fruit so long as he is joined to that society [of

the monastery]; and he complains that he is cut off from spiritual gain, and is of no use in the place.[17]

In his cell, he has no company, no cosmic purpose to achieve.

The monk begins to notice how slowly the time passes. He devises plans to get busy. He will visit the sick and the widow. This, he tells himself, would be a work of real, measurable "piety," something to assuage the fear of his own insignificance.

> It would be a most excellent thing to get what is needful for her who is neglected and despised by her own kinsfolk; and . . . he ought piously to devote his time to these things instead of staying *uselessly* and with no profit in his cell.[18]

Surely the monk is justified for leaving off prayer and study. He wants to make a difference in the world!

But Cassian asks us to look closer, to notice the monk's attempts at escape. The monk, Cassian insists, suffers from sloth, this "battering ram" of acedia. If he is not driven to slumber, he will be driven to flight. Either he will fail the efforts required for devoted prayer and diligent study, or he will distract himself with self-justified busyness. Either way, it will not be worship he offers to God. It will not be ministry he offers to the world. It will be violation of his vocation, the life charge given to him by God. "Vocation is never perceived as a personal achievement or goal," writes John Swinton in *Becoming Friends of Time*. "It is not an individual search for the fulfillment of our own destiny."[19]

When I complete a five-year travel history for a Canadian citizenship application, I count scores of days I've been away from home to speak at churches or conferences. I remember how I've never entirely forgiven myself for missing my daughter's very important clarinet audition in March 2019, when she was applying to college. It didn't matter that the audition was scheduled a month in advance, that my event was booked a year ahead.

"Frenetic disciples may get a lot of things done," explains theologian John Swinton, "but in doing a lot of things they may miss the very things that God is doing."[20] Sometimes you leave your cell to heed the voice of God. And sometimes you leave it to be convinced you count.

You can be a bird in noisy, frantic flight—and tell yourself it's God's errand.

Heroes Need Not Apply

"Know that the LORD, he is God! It is he who made us, and we are his."[21] As I unreliably begin the practice of fixed-hour prayer in the early months of 2020, I'm using a guide called *The Divine Hours*. These are the months I feel thwarted in the desire to make myself *useful*, months I don't travel to speak, months I rarely leave the house. These are not months for making any noticeable difference in the world. They are months of dailyness, of routine chores. As I pray the hours, I start to notice that each of the daily offices begins with the invitation to praise God.

> The LORD is King: let the people tremble.
> I will offer you a freewill sacrifice and praise your
>   name, O LORD, for it is good.

> Come, let us sing to the LORD; let us shout for joy
> to the Rock of our salvation.[22]

I quickly learn you can't recognize your resistance to praise until you're led forcibly to it, breakfast, lunch, and dinner. Until you've watched yourself struggle to *give God five minutes of your day.* I had rationalizations for this, of course. This resistance to *blessing the LORD, O my soul* was not a resistance to worship; I just felt the urgency of the day's business pressing in. I just needed to get things done.

But maybe that's part of the point of worship, that it de-centers us and our work, that it enthrones God and God's work instead.

Worship counters the aspirations of productivity by which we measure time's value. Worship is what's extravagantly figured, in the Old Testament, in all those regular trips to Jerusalem, all those routine feasts, all those animals offered, the smell of burning flesh rising to God. To see worship as pilgrimage, performed year after year, is to see that worship has little to do with progress, at least as we tend to think of that word. It doesn't move us forward, doesn't get us ahead. Doesn't finish something, once and for all. Worship is a wholly inefficient act.

I would prefer a more heroic part in the drama of life. I like leading roles, encores. It's probably why I've liked time management books: because there's such strong appeal in earning the admiration of others for all you do with so little time. In Melissa Gregg's reading of the genre, she sees time management books as recruitment for superhumans, as "a form of training through which workers become capable of the ever more daring acts of solitude and ruthlessness necessary to produce career competence."[23] The industry tends to feature the feats of people like Merlin Mann, who addressed Google employees in 2007.

At first, Mann was enamored of email as a new technology. Soon, however, he found himself overwhelmed. Mann then pioneered the technique of Inbox Zero and sold his story, one that, according to Gregg, "charts a recognizable course. 'You think I'm not like you, but listen. I had your problem. I overcame it. Here's how. Copy me and see that you can be successful, too.'"[24] Mann became the kind of guru and motivational speaker we lap up in our thirst to perform spectacular feats of productivity.

All that circus juggling ended for Mann, however, when he realized years later that writing about productivity was forcing him to abandon the priorities he most cherished. "I'm mostly out of the productivity racket these days," Mann told Oliver Burkeman in an interview for *The Guardian*. "If you're just using efficiency to jam more and more stuff into your day . . . well, how would you ever know that that's working?"[25]

We like our heroes. We especially like our Christian ones. Laura Fabrycky is the author of *Keys to Bonhoeffer's Haus*, and over the past several years, across continents, she has become a friend. I love her book for many reasons. Perhaps I love it most for the way it offers a window into the life of Bonhoeffer as someone who was as human as he was heroic.

To read other biographies of Bonhoeffer, one is easily persuaded that when he was murdered by the Nazi regime in 1944, his life was inimitable. We could not imitate his clarity, and we could not imitate his courage. But this is exactly how we must *not* understand Bonhoeffer, writes Laura, who served as a guide at the Bonhoeffer Haus in Berlin during her family's three-year diplomatic assignment.

It was during her time at the house that Laura came to a more complicated understanding of Bonhoeffer, especially his decision to return to Germany from the United States in 1939, a decision that would seal his fate. Bonhoeffer struggled to hear God's voice and discern a clear sense of calling. His faithfulness—human, imperfect—was not a measure of heroism but the habit of drinking water from that deep, invisible river of Good.

Bonhoeffer made his second visit to New York in the summer of 1939 with noble intentions. He sought not just safety but the "prospect of a university position and a lecture tour in the United States and many opportunities to communicate about the situation in Nazi Germany to the world."[26] He could be sure of a certain *usefulness* in America. But he was unsettled. He could not leave behind the sense he owed a debt of personal responsibility to Germany and its future.

It was during this short summer stay in New York that Bonhoeffer recorded insights from his daily readings in *Die Losungen,* which were pairs of "watchwords," or pairs of verses, one from the Old Testament, one from the New. It was a season during which Bonhoeffer was riven with uncertainty about God's calling in his life. Should he stay in New York? Or return home?

In the initial tours she gave at the house, Laura shaped a narrative around a single point of decision—and the blinding light of a single watchword. Soon, however, she understood that this must be corrected. "There was not one watchword, no single fortune-cookie paper that cast magic lamplight on his heroic path."[27] Instead, what guided Bonhoeffer was a long history of formation: in a community of belonging, such as his family and the seminary he ran briefly for the Confessing Church; in his private spiritual practices like Scripture meditation and praying the Psalms.

As Laura puts it, prayer was for Bonhoeffer an orienting force in understanding how he might offer his life to God and in service to his neighbor. For one, prayer prevented Bonhoeffer from falling prey to megalomania, this lust to make a cosmic difference in the world. Two, prayer also rescued him from acedia, or civic sloth, a sin that seemed endemic to German society in the Third Reich, as people failed to find the will to care about their Jewish neighbors, or even about the fate of the nation itself.

> Prayer kept the heavy weights of his responsibilities from crushing him entirely. It was the great stream in which he could connect his own life with God's, his solitary and peripatetic life with a larger community, and keep a sharp watch on the needs and injustices around him. Prayer offered him solace and simultaneously plunged him more deeply into the needs of the world.[28]

Prayer, in other words, called him from the world and summoned him back to it. None of Bonhoeffer's spiritual practices, Laura writes, offered "an escape from life; they offer[ed] a way to *avoid* escaping it—a way back from stone into flesh."[29]

For Bonhoeffer, prayer swung like the doors at Fall Creek Abbey, opening wide to receive the world and its needs—and finding times for turning the lock, shutting out every other voice but God's.

A Case for Extravagance

"Calling doesn't come preassembled," I say to a group of people gathered at the Boorams'. I'm in town for a conference, and Beth and David have organized us to celebrate the launch of my most recent book. We are sitting in the living room of Fall Creek Abbey, and I am tracing my journey from French and English major to teacher to mother to writer.

"We all want to know what we have to offer in the world. And we want to know that whatever we offer, whatever we attempt, we'll know exactly what to do and how it's going to turn out." I wait, then continue, thinking of how many billboards, how many neon signs I'd waited on to avoid vocation's risks.

"Unfortunately, God never says, 'I'm going to keep you from failure.' We have to walk by faith, not sight." I know that I am failing to give the reassurances many in this crowd want, the reassurances I myself have often demanded, but I also know it's faith we must exercise to hear the voice of God; faith we must exercise to trust others to affirm our gifts, to brave scary opportunities, to risk our inadequacies, and to rely on God to make good even of our mistakes. In my case at least, my vocation, or calling, took shape in initially dim light.

I wasn't going to be a writer, I tell this group. Yes, I grew up with a father who was a writer. Yes, I grew up with a family that pilgrimaged to the library every week, a habit that taught me to love books. Yes, in secret I might have entertained fantasies about writing, and yes, alongside raising my children I took occasional freelance devotional projects. But this wasn't confidence. This wasn't clarity. These were hints.

One thing that might have been especially difficult, I confessed to this group, were my impoverished models of vocation. While growing up I'd lacked richly diverse examples of the variety of faithful lives women might offer to God in the world. Thanks to my friendship with Laura, however, I'd been more recently introduced to the Beguines, an informally organized group of religious women in the Middle Ages.

When author Laura Swan visited the Belgian city of Bruges, her tour guide told her that the Beguines were "pious old women praying and doing good works until they died."[30] Unlike monks or nuns, the Beguines didn't take official religious vows or live in the countryside, farming the land. Their communities were established, starting around the year 1200, in the urban centers of Europe.

Many of the Beguines, like me and like Laura, engaged forms of writing as acts of vocation. Their writings included "dictated visions, poetry and prayers, some correspondence, as well as *vitae*." These writings also included biblical commentaries, sermons, and lists of martyrs and saints.[31] In my research on the Beguines, I also learned these women were patrons of the arts; they commissioned not just statuary, like pietàs, but also psalters, or medieval books of hours.

One day I found myself spending hours poring over the vivid pictures of the thirteenth century Psalter of Lambert, published on the website of the British Library. There are pages dedicated to each month of the calendar—the month's feasts and its particular form of labor. (May, I learn, is the month for hawking.) Throughout the pages of the Psalms, which is the principal text of this small devotional book, are illustrations of Christ's life—because "Christ is the subject of the entire book, for He is the Blessed Man of Psalm 1."[32]

In the upper left-hand corner of the page where Psalm 109 opens, there is the figure of God the Father holding up Christ on the cross, over whose head a dove hovers. "Be not silent, O God of my praise! For wicked and deceitful mouths are opened against me."[33] Other pages are dedicated to various scenes of Christ's life: the flight into Egypt, Herod and the massacre of the Innocents, Christ's temptation, Christ healing a blind man, the Transfiguration. On the opening page of Psalm 137, doubting Thomas, cloaked in red, kneels before Christ and reaches to put his finger in the hole in Jesus's side. "By the waters of Babylon, there we sat down and wept."[34] On another page, birds are perched along the script that flowers into the margins.

I am finding so much indulgence here, in these saturated reds and blues and greens, so much expense in these pages applied with gold. Medieval psalters were so precious that they were frequently named in Beguine wills. These small books, or breviaries, make me think of the bottle of perfume broken over Jesus's feet by a woman— this "waste," according to Judas. I fear books like these are the extravagances we are no longer willing to offer when efficiency is our highest good.

Efficiency: how often my own vocational efforts have derailed in pursuit of this "good" whose cousins are hurry and haste. "The lazy way is the long way," I've been telling my kids all their lives, when they've been tempted to cut corners. But I see that corner cutting is exactly what I've done with another writing project, weeks ago. I had wanted the assignment done quickly and effortlessly, and I'd tried sparing myself the rigors of hard work.

It is the extravagance of a poem that shows me this. On a recent Sabbath, I give myself a little more time in my chair, and after my morning Scripture reading, I open Wendell Berry's book of Sabbath poems called *A Timbered Choir*. On this particular Sunday, the last poem from 1980 takes me by the collar and gives me a gentle shake. It figures a field worn out by the diseased efforts of human beings.

I know the warning I'm meant to have in these lines of verse: *greed and sloth / did bad work that this thicket now conceals.* [35] It makes me remember what I'd read about another deadly sin, the sin of vainglory, described in Rebecca DeYoung's *Glittering Vices*. Vainglory, as this greed for self-glory, is another corruption of vocation. The antidotes she prescribed were, for one, silence and solitude. "Stepping out of the spotlight and cultivating habits of silence and solitude may at first make us feel lonely, even bereft."[36]

It is noteworthy how many of the seven deadly sins have a particular temporal bent. They're impatient, they're hurried. "Vainglory," explains DeYoung, "serves those who prefer to take a shortcut to these real goods [of virtue]. Why work at actually being pious, or face difficulty and the possibility of failure, if we can pull off the mere reputation more easily?"[37] *Greed and sloth / did bad work that this thicket now conceals.* I feel that I've been X-rayed, that the film has been held against the light.

I copy a couple of lines of this Sabbath poem into the margin of my planner and make them a prayer for the week, lines that call me to "exactitude of thought" and "skill of hand" and "the clouded mercy of the sky."[38] What is summoned, simultaneously, is hard work and trust.

On Monday morning, I spread the pages of my writing project across the dining room table. I take scissors to them. I resolve exactitude. I pray for skill, for patience. Then I imagine rainfall and a brimming river, trees planted nearby. I think of quiet mornings at Fall Creek Abbey and mornings in my chair, receiving a daily version of Bonhoeffer's watchwords. I remember the obscure legacy of the Beguines, lost to history until only more recently.

With a view of the street, I listen and write. And writing, on this quiet morning, is my slow act of worship.

TO CONSIDER

Who, in your life, has modeled faithful vocation, and what have you learned from them?

Can you identify temptations to short-circuit or even entirely avoid the efforts required to faithfully offer your gifts to God and to your neighbor?

How can you begin to understand the callings of your season of life as expressions of praise?

TO PRAY

God, you are worthy of gifts far greater than my offerings, and by the sacrifice of Jesus Christ, you make my obedient worship possible. Take all that I have and all that I am, and use them for the glory of Christ and the good of my neighbor. When I am tempted to avoid the work required to cultivate my skills, when I forget the importance of hidden disciplines to cultivate my character, call me back to you.

Wait

As we wait on God's promise keeping, we remain patient and learn to endure with hope.

Pandemic months might be measured in the small kitchen appliances I begin buying. The espresso machine. The burr coffee grinder. The single-serve smoothie blender. After months of indecision, finally, the large electric ice cream maker, which Ryan warns we'll never use. "What's that?" Ryan asks when it arrives two days later. I heave it onto the kitchen island, not wanting to tell him.

As if to prove my ice cream maker has not been an unnecessary purchase, I make ice cream almost every Saturday. Every time, it is a full-day operation. By 8:00 a.m., I am stirring the custard base on the stove. After it cools in the refrigerator until at least noon, I churn it on the counter for an hour, then freeze it again. My kids grow to understand they cannot ask at 4:00 p.m. if we are having ice cream that night. "I've got to get it started by breakfast, remember?" For months, I work to perfect the vanilla base. I compare online recipes. I try fewer eggs. I try less cream. I try more milk.

This spate of small appliance purchases, delivered in days by Amazon, betrays the privilege I enjoy in the global crisis. I am not an essential worker. I have disposable income and discretionary time.

It's not just kitchen gadgetry that testifies to my privilege. As our children transition to virtual schooling, they are outfitted with every needed technology to make the shift, including connection to the internet, which many Toronto public school students lack. As I read in *Toronto Life*, 38 percent of households in my city have "slow, patchy internet access" and 150,000 city residents have no home internet at all. Even for those who do have regular internet access, one survey of low-income Canadians "found that 35 percent have made sacrifices to pay for [the service], including skipping food, medication and transit to cover their internet bills."[1]

My friend Constance, a single mother and recent immigrant to Canada, has internet access, thank God. She also has two of the seventeen thousand devices loaned by the Toronto district Catholic school board. Still, she has too few hands to help all three of her children, all younger than eight, to log into their Google classrooms and "attend" school. When I deliver groceries to her house weekly in the early months of Toronto's first lockdown, I notice the exhausted hunch of her shoulders as I stand on the landing outside her front door.

COVID suffering has not abided fairness. I make ice cream as people go hungry. As people lose their jobs, America's 650-odd billionaires get $1.2 trillion richer. Jeff Bezos, founder and executive chairman of Amazon, sees his own personal fortune rise by upward of $86 million. Shares of Amazon rise 87 percent between January 2020 and April 2021, though frontline Amazon workers watch their earnings increase by a mere 7 percent.[2]

I could join the collective complaint against Amazon, set to become the largest private employer in the United States in the next year or two. But that would be to participate in the widespread irony: that we subscribe to a world where Amazon scurries to our door with tens of thousands of daily essentials and groceries in a matter of hours.

When Amazon delivers my slightly dented ice cream maker, I am, of course, too impatient to bother returning it.

Employee productivity is a key component to Amazon's success. The company rigorously tracks the performance of their employees. Amazon knows how fast their employees pack, how long they pause. Too much TOT, or *time off task,* can be reason for dismissal, even if it means you've simply gone to the bathroom or tried troubleshooting a problem.

David Niekerk, a former vice president for human resources at Amazon, admitted to the *New York Times* that Bezos has structured ways to deliberately incent the company's hourly workers to leave after several years. "What he would say is that our nature as humans is to expend as little energy as possible to get what we want or need," explained Niekerk.[3] Amazon would use up the best energies of their employees, then retire them early. At the rate Amazon burns through employees, estimates are they will need between eight and ten million people to apply every year—or 5 percent of the American workforce.

My Amazon purchase history reads as a kind of pandemic record. On March 15, 2020, I order three volumes of *The Divine Hours,* the fixed-hour prayer manual edited by Phyllis Tickle. On March 21, bathroom cleaner, rubber gloves, garbage bags, and hand lotion are delivered. On April 22, after my daughter has complained of soreness caused by the hours spent sitting in her chair for virtual school, I buy a cushion for her desk chair. On April 24, I buy my youngest son, Colin, a portable laptop stand. On April 27, Ryan buys an oversized TV he's been eyeing. Several months later, my husband places orders for the books his counselor has recommended: on burnout, on friendship, on marriage, and David Brooks's *The Second Mountain.*

Amazon stocks the house in record time, rewarding the consumer tic.

I don't wait. On the ice cream maker, that is.

Many months later, it sits in a box in the storage room of our basement. "Why don't you make ice cream anymore?" Colin keeps asking me.

I am tired at the thought.

Not the Before, Not Yet the After

God's way with us is waiting.

A friend said this to me many years ago, and given the biblical evidence, it certainly seems true. How often has

God spoken promises to his people, then asked them to wait on their fulfillment?

For starters, there are the childless years of the matriarchs. The years of bleeding, pleading, God seeming to be deaf. The central redemptive promise of Genesis has to do with the "seed," this offspring of Eve who will crush the head of the serpent—yet Sarah, Rebekah, and Rachel endure seasons of infertility. When God tells Abraham he will make him a mighty nation, he also informs him there will be four hundred intervening years of affliction. After God finally delivers his people from Egyptian slavery, Israel demonstrates mistrust on the other side of the Red Sea and is condemned to forty years of wilderness wandering. Many centuries later, between Malachi's prophecy of the second "Elijah" and the first-century firebrand son of Zechariah, four hundred long years of silence echo.

No, God does not deliver on his promises with Amazon efficiency. Rather, it seems God might be accused of slowness, of dragging his heels, of spending too much *time off task*. It certainly seems true that he minds waiting far less than we do; that he has baked waiting into the project of the kingdom, which Jesus compared to a mustard seed and yeast. These are images of time elapsing while God grows something slowly and nearly imperceptibly. Yes, God does as he pleases, the Bible tells us—and it seems, from many of the stories, that he pleases to take his good ole time.

Human beings have always been impatient with this God running behind our timetables. We hate uncertainty. We despise the feeling of fumbling in the dark. We can feel abandoned by God in seasons of waiting. If Uber Eats can get dinner to my door in a half hour, why should God ever choose delay? That's the sentiment of many psalms of lament, anyway: "How long, O LORD? Will you forget me forever?"[4]

I am mostly a rookie in waiting. I am the woman who buys small kitchen appliances with alacrity, who suffers shipping delays as sources of real grief. For my friend Constance, waiting is more real, more dire.

I'm not simply speaking of her long commute on public transportation, involving a transfer between a bus and a streetcar, to get her boys to and from school. For more than a year, I drove Constance and her three young boys to immigration appointments as they fought deportation. Those were long mornings of waiting to be called back into a small room, passing babies between us and her pro bono lawyer.

After one visit to the Canadian immigration office, when the officer told Constance she would need to procure passports for her Canadian-born babies, I remember our multiple treks, on foot, to the passport office, each of us with a baby strapped to our chest. We'd tramped through the rain to get the necessary paperwork notarized, and when we'd arrived back at the office a second time, we took our number: D523.

They were currently taking A213 and A214.

Waiting is a habit difficult to form. It is difficult to form with a screaming baby strapped to your chest, and it is difficult to form when instantaneity is so highly prized, when technology accelerates time and our expectations of it. But if it's true that God's way with us is waiting, then waiting is a habit of the Christian life. We will have to content ourselves with God's timekeeping, however slow it seems.

Pandemic life has been liminal life: not the before and not yet the after. And maybe this is to say that it has plunged us into the experience of Christian time, which poet W. H. Auden has called the "time being." It's a time that calls for waiting, for watching. Though God himself stands outside of time, we are held firmly in its iron grip.

Christ will come again to judge the living and the dead— and we are waiting on this day, when the world is put to rights, when sin and death are finally put under the feet of Jesus, when the church of God is presented to Christ as his radiant bride. These are promises in seed form: certain and not yet harvested.

Christian time is patient time. It looks like Thursday morning at my house, when my dog sits at the window, her paws on the back of the couch. Thursday is the day for her walk with the neighborhood pack, and she is waiting for that white Jeep Cherokee to pull up in front of the house and her favorite dogwalker, Suzanne, to alight from its driver's side.

Waiting is a function of hope.

In her collection of Advent sermons, pastor and theologian Fleming Rutledge reminds us that the church doesn't live the world's time. Our time, as Christians, isn't only hurry and haste, only productivity and material progress. Mark 13, she writes, provides us with a story to illustrate the waiting and watching that God's people are called to.

In this story, Jesus tells his listeners that there is still more waiting ahead of God's people as they anticipate the second advent of the Lord. Jesus explains that it will be as if a man has taken a long journey, leaving his servants in charge of the house. They won't know the time of his return home, and it will be tempting to find themselves drowsy. "Stay awake," Jesus commands, "for you do not know when the master of the house will come, in the evening, or at midnight, or when the rooster crows, or in the morning."[5]

Don't let him find you failing to watch for that white Jeep Cherokee to pull up in front of the house.

When the Cup of Endurance Runs Over

In 2020, friendships between people I dearly love break down. There is hemorrhaging, as if a major artery has been cut. There is suffering and sin, and the woundedness is not easily staunched. To change the metaphor, you can't find the beginnings or the ends of this tangle, and no matter how hard you work the knot of blame, your too-fat fingers cannot assign it.

Let me be clear that the misfortune is not the conflict. No, conflict is a risk of belonging. An inevitability, I'd even say. With all the admonitions in the Bible to get along, to forgive, to make peace, conflict is assumed. The greater misfortune becomes the impatience. People forget love is a project of forbearance, a waiting with and waiting out. If transformation is slow in us, why can't it also be slow in others?

When virus fears force mediation of this conflict online, relationships fray even further. Soon enough, forgiveness is withheld, justice is demanded, grievances are published on social media. The situation is just as Simone Weil describes in *Waiting on God*: "Every time that we put forth some effort and the equivalent of this effort does not come back to us in the form of some visible fruit, we have a sense of false balance and emptiness which makes us think we have been cheated."[6]

There are sides to take—and to me at least, none of them are obvious.

In these factious months, what strangely comforts me are the apocalyptic visions recorded in Revelation, which I discover when my Bible reading plan lands me there. There are angels and dragons, broken seals, and an on-slaught of disasters. The sky is rolled back like a scroll, and the world's inhabitants take cover from the all-seeing, all-knowing, always-reigning God. "Fall on us and hide us from the face of him who is seated on the throne."[7]

Revelation's terror—and comfort—is the sure knowledge that God is on the throne. To hear the chorus in heaven resounding in praise to God—"just and true are your ways"—is to remember to cast all hope on God's impartiality.[8] I cannot always know how to decide these things, but God knows and will.

In January 2021, I am attending a writing workshop, and we are reading Martin Luther King's 1963 "Letter from Birmingham Jail." Eight white clergymen had accused the black civil right's activist of his "unwise and untimely" march in Birmingham, when he defied a court order and led protesters, without a permit, to boycott white-owned stores.

"I am in Birmingham because injustice is here," King responds. "Just as the prophets of the eighth century BC left their villages and carried their 'thus saith the Lord' far beyond the boundaries of their home towns . . . I am compelled to carry the gospel of freedom beyond my own home town."[9] The clergymen had wanted King to exercise patience, to allow time for the newly elected mayor of Birmingham to respond to the movement's grievances.

In his letter, King explains that patience has been exhausted. We've waited through slavery, he writes. We've waited through lynchings, through segregation. "For years now I have heard the word 'Wait!' It rings in the ear of every Negro with piercing familiarity. This 'Wait' has almost always meant 'Never.' We must come to see, with one of our distinguished jurists, that 'justice too long delayed is justice denied.'"[10]

"There comes a time when the cup of endurance runs over," King adds. I think of my friends, their brimming cups of anger. Their patience has long been exhausted, and I am (at least partially) sympathetic to their unwillingness to wait.

Waiting may very well run its course, and when it does, impatience can sometimes give way to something good—like persistence. Met with injustice, cruelty, abuse, neglect, someone finally says "Enough!" This can be good and right, and it's an impulse I see affirmed in the parable of the persistent widow and the unjust judge. This woman would not abandon her case, despite how the judge continued to send her away. When he finally did agree to give her justice against her adversary, it was not because his heart had softened, only that he'd grown irritated by her pestering. "Though I neither fear God nor respect man, yet because this widow keeps bothering me, I will give her justice, so that she will not beat me down by her continual coming."[11] In the Bible, wisdom is characterized by goodness—and goodness by justice. Goodness can't help its intolerance and active opposition to evil. Goodness can indeed have protest in its blood. It did in Birmingham. It did in Soweto. After the killings of Michael Brown and Breonna Taylor and George Floyd, it did in Ferguson and Louisville and Minneapolis.

Sadly, though, sometimes protest and pestering and persistence are not enough to defeat the powers of evil. Sometimes injustice, on this side of the veil, seems to prevail. Sometimes innocent lambs are led to slaughter, and the Son of God is betrayed into the hands of sinners. What to do when justice is delayed? Persist, yes. Pester, yes. And also *endure*.

Endurance is an expression of faithful waiting. It requires remembering the real length of God's time.

Endure isn't the meaning I had initially seen in a familiar passage, John 15, where Jesus compares himself to a vine and his followers to vine branches. "Abide in me," he urges his disciples in verse 4, according to the ESV and the RSV, two popular translations of the Bible. "Remain in me," he says in the NIV translation, "as I also remain in you." But as I read further, arriving at verse 16, I begin to see that another meaning might be in mind beyond the contemplative posture I thought Jesus was commending: "I chose you and appointed you that you should go and bear fruit and that your fruit should *abide*." What seems clear here is the sense of fruit enduring and persevering. Waiting, in other words.

Endurance is the virtue to exercise in liminal time. It is mettle formed by heat. Endurance is the capacity to wait and wait out: to remain, rest, persevere, and abide. It is a virtue made necessary in a world that resists repair and restoration.

I can't help but think that in an Amazon world, where gratification is delivered fast and without friction, endurance is a virtue that runs in short supply. I can't help but think that sin today is often about the failure to wait. Our greed. Our lust. Our envy. Our vainglory. Our wrath. Our gluttony. Even our pride and our sloth.

Hurry corrupts the means to ends we can't stand to postpone.

A Season of Dormancy

Saint Monica knew the habit of waiting. Monica is the mother of Saint Augustine, the brilliant and rhetorically gifted young son for whom she prayed many years, "suffering birth pangs, so to speak, again every time she saw [him] leave the true path and move away from [God.]"[12]

I am reading about Saint Monica in the last remaining "before" days: before we are sent home from vacation and the world takes unrecognizable shape. I like the book *On the Road with Saint Augustine*, even if I don't especially like how James K. A. Smith has articulated the difficulty children have with their mothers and their "suffocating embrace."[13] His words hit dangerously close to home.

When Monica was especially laid low by thoughts of this dissolute son of hers, God gave this waiting mother a dream that seemed meant to allay her fears about Augustine's spiritual future. Still, it took nine years for Monica to see God's fulfillment of this dream. Nine years of waiting.

Monica waited and prayed—and prayed and waited. And though she had the reassurance of the dream, she wasn't afraid to ask Ambrose, Bishop of Milan, to talk to Augustine and "refute [his] errors and correct [his] evil doctrines and teach [him] good ones." When Ambrose refused, Monica begged and pleaded. She wept, "begging and with floods of tears, asking [Ambrose] to see [her son] and debate with [him]." This is a woman whose desperation I recognize. "He was now irritated and a little vexed and said: 'Go away from me: as you live, it cannot be that the son of these tears should perish.'"[14]

Saint Monica, writes Smith, represents the cult of weeping, waiting mothers, those mothers who can't sleep because of their children's wandering ways. Mothers, like me, lying awake after a child's betrayal of trust. The story of Monica isn't just a story of historical curiosity for Smith, however. It's his own wife, Deanna, whom he finds weeping in the Basilica di Sant'Agostino, beside Monica's tomb, when they are visiting Rome. Deanna is holding a prayer card, a prayer to God and also to this fierce mother Monica of many tears: to God, for grace; to Saint Monica, for help for "all those who can't find the path of sanctity."[15]

I don't believe in praying to saints—but I could be tempted as I first read these prayers. So could my friends Jill and Esther, with whom I share the prayer as we navigate the icy paths of a Toronto ravine, zipped in our parkas. Praying for our children together, we are members of this cult of Saint Monica, mothers who wait and watch and weep.

All this praying for our children makes me think of the waiting and watching Israel did on the shores of the Red

Sea, in the moments before God's wind drove a dry path through the water: "Fear not, stand firm, and see the salvation of the LORD, which he will work for you today. For the Egyptians whom you see today, you shall never see again. The LORD will fight for you, and you have only to be silent."[16] It reminds me that waiting is not always inaction or excuse. Waiting can be a profound act of trust in God's timing.

Nothing, I begin to think, is wasted in waiting. No, this is where faith is put together, limb by limb. Waiting is a furnace for endurance. Waiting may seem unproductive, but it is like the careful cultivation of a vineyard.

When I visit a couple of internet sites on grape growing, I learn a new vineyard won't have usable grapes until its third year. Until that point, any clusters must be pruned in order to strengthen the roots. I read that the key is patience. You can't overly water—by a drip hose, for example, though it would surely seem more efficient. A healthy vine needs deprivation in order to send its roots deeper. And in the fall, you have to cut back on water even further in order to send the plant into its winter dormancy. Every grape gathered is a product of time.

"To all things there is a season," another vineyard website reminds readers, channeling the spirit of Ecclesiastes. Spring is budbreak. There are new shoots, and the extra buds you've left from winter as an insurance policy must be thinned. Summer is fast growth. Irrigate. Keep training and manually positioning the shoots on the trellis. Thin the fruit so as to not exhaust the vines. Fall is harvest. Beware of predators. Winter is the season for pruning, for considering the growth of the past season, the vine's current condition, the desired growth for next season. In winter, water is scarce. But beneath the surface of the soil, the invisible legs of the vine lengthen and fortify.

A series of winters, a series of waiting seasons: this is what holds the vine in the storm.

God's Patient Waiting

We think we are waiting on God, but it appears God, this patient vinedresser of human lives, is also waiting on us. At least this is what I notice in a session of spiritual direction, when Beth reads from an unfamiliar translation of Isaiah 30:18:

> Meanwhile, the Eternal One yearns to give you
> grace and boundless compassion;
> that's why He waits.
> For the Eternal is a God of justice.
> Those inclined toward Him, waiting for His
> help, will find happiness.[17]

What is this waiting that God does, I wonder? Does he wait on our readiness for his gifts? Does he wait on the humility or courage required for receiving them? Maybe he waits for us to recognize our dependence, to finally cry out for help. Maybe he waits until our eyes are rimmed in red, until our tears flood like Saint Monica's. I only know that God's waiting is a longing, a yearning, a hoping all things for and in us. It is the sight of the prodigal father, his nose pressed against the pane, his eyes on the road.

God is waiting on every fractured family and friendship. God is waiting on sheep wandering from his fold. With untiring love, God is waiting on this groaning world. "In a very deep sense," says Fleming Rutledge, "the entire Christian life in this world is lived in Advent, between the first and second comings of the Lord, in the midst of the tension between things the way they are and things the way they ought to be."[18] Advent is the in-between time, and what's needed for waiting, I begin to think, isn't knowledge but strength. *Persevere in me, as I persevere in you. If you endure in me, and my words endure in you, ask whatever you wish, and it will be done for you.*[19]

Endurance is the word I meditate on when I travel to Ohio to help my mother and stepfather move into a larger apartment, months before our move to be closer to them. Recently, my stepfather came home from a five-day hospital stay with oxygen, and the compressor and its snaking cord made it difficult to navigate their cramped one-bedroom space. A change was needed, and I was needed to help them make it. I am good in these moments of crisis: when tasks are screaming, when the clock is ticking, when what is needed is furious motion. All my life, I've been training to get things done.

On the trip, I take with me an Ecclesiastes commentary my friend has recommended. *Living Life Backward* by David Gibson proves to be a fitting companion for these long days of sorting through cabinets and closets and packing my minivan for multiple trips to Goodwill; this week has at its very center the vanity of human life. During the week, I grow frustrated with my mother for her incapacity to be of meaningful help—and angry with myself for such heartless frustration. A woman from the assisted living facility overhears my loud irritation at one point when the door to my mother's apartment stands open. Later, in the elevator, she reminds me my mother is "a very kind lady."

Productivity, I can see soberly, is not the same thing as kindness.

After five days, and with the help of my stepsister and her husband, I have my mother and my stepfather mostly settled. The beds are made, the boxes are unpacked, and with more help from my high school friend and her husband, we even have pictures hung on the walls. But what I haven't done, despite the long hours I record at the front desk of their assisted living facility, signing in every morning and out every night, is *fix* this situation. My mother is still forgetting things in short spans of time. My stepfather is still physically declining—and hanging his head low because of the unwanted changes in his body. Even a long visit to the bank doesn't untangle the complicated financial matters I hoped to attend to. "What is crooked cannot be made straight," writes the Teacher in Ecclesiastes. "What is lacking cannot be counted."[20] It seems aging is one of those crooked things, giving way to absences and aches that are hard to count.

"Do not be surprised to find yourself in a frustrating situation from which you cannot escape by means of controlling it," I read in Gibson's commentary, sitting at my friend's kitchen table one morning. She has been hosting me this week, every night listening to my laments about the used plastic bags and mustard packets my mother has been squirreling away. "Not everything can be fixed! Not everything is a problem to be solved.

Some things must be borne, must be suffered and endured."[21] I have never wanted to believe in my impotence, of course. It's why waiting is always so impossibly hard, because it requires me to believe God is acting even when I am not.

In the dark quiet of this January morning, looking onto my friend's shared backyard, I notice there is not a single house illumined. Mothers and fathers, sons and daughters: they're all sleeping. This small lot of humanity, like Saint Monica, dreams. Whether they mean to or not, I imagine they practice the faith of sleep. They close their eyes and believe the galaxies will not career off course, that planets and moons and distant stars will not rain from the sky simply because they stopped watching.

Drinking my coffee, I listen for sounds of my friend's son waking to catch the school bus. I think of the psalmist who speaks of the night watchman keeping awake in vain. "Unless the LORD watches over the city," he reminds sleepless people like me.[22]

Waiting for the sun, I drink my coffee. And believe, somehow, that God is waiting too.

TO CONSIDER

What has you impatient right now, and how will you wait well?

How has privilege insulated you from the irritations of waiting? How has injustice eroded your willingness to wait?

What will it look like for you to trust God where justice appears to be thwarted?

What suffering must simply be borne in this season of life, and what help can you ask from God and his people?

God, you are slow to anger and abounding in steadfast love. It's clear your patience is expressed as forgiveness and mercy. Help me to remember your patient waiting on this groaning world, and let it transform my anger, my irritation, my impatience. I trust that even when justice seems slow, in your hands it is sure. Give me the power to persevere in suffering and hold fast to hope.

Practice

As we keep at the tedium of faithfulness, we commit ourselves to the habits of a long, slow obedience.

When businesses reopen after Toronto's first lockdown, I discover a small shop in Toronto's east end that sells houseplants. As a civic duty, of course, I start buying them: succulents, a banana plant, a ZZ plant, a Chinese money plant, a peperomia.

My mother was a plant grower. I remember our own house feeling a bit forested, especially with the large, frizzy fern my mother kept transplanting into bigger and bigger pots and moving to different corners of the house. I remember African violets and a fast-growing jade plant. I remember hens and chicks multiplying in pots on the porch. I can see the red bloom of the Christmas cactus, the white blooms on the shamrock. On Saturdays, I watched my mother fill an old milk jug with water and dump in a small scoop of fertilizer, then travel from plant to plant to plant. On drizzly summer days, I watched her lug all the plants outside and bathe them in rain.

After Ryan and I were married, I brought home our first English ivy and set it atop our bookcase in the living room of our one-bedroom apartment. I didn't know if the ivy liked shade or direct sun. I didn't know if it liked to be regularly watered or dried out in between. I only knew I liked its spindly limbs cascading like a waterfall over our old college textbooks. Months later, when those leafy legs grew webbed, I couldn't have known the ivy had been infected with spider mites. I just threw it away and replaced it with another. And another. And then another. After that fourth ivy, I took a hiatus from plant growing.

I have never really liked the strict regimen of plant care. I feel the imposition of the regular, systematic attention plants require. I have wanted them to grow unassisted by me, to feel grateful for my irregular affections. I have wanted it to be sufficient if, after weeks of neglect, I remembered them like old friends I'd forgotten to call. During our cloistered pandemic months, however, I began to resent these mundane demands less. I could watch my new plants like patients. I could sit vigil, deciding just when they needed to be watered or moved or turned.

What I had in the crisis, in other words, was time: regular, plodding, predictable, ordinary time. Days after successive days, weeks after successive weeks, even months after successive months. I could perform the regular faithfulness of plant care—the kind of regular faithfulness that sets to flight the noonday demon of acedia, or sloth, this vice that tires of efforts needing to be repeated, over and over again. In the fourth century, Evagrius prescribed repetition and regularity as antidote for this deadly sin: "Set a measure for yourself in everything that you do, and don't turn from it until you've reached the goal," the monk wrote.[1]

Monastic men and women understood that persevering faithfulness, which is to say *practice*, countered the vice of acedia. If acedia was "resistance to the demands of love," it could be battled by noticing one's desire for escape and willfully taking up burdens instead.[2] Burdens in the form of regular spiritual practices—like prayer, fasting, generosity, and study. Burdens in the form of ordinary human life—like housework, conflict management, and care for the sick, the young, the dying.

The important thing is remembering that faithful life is not an instant home makeover show.

"What we need most in countering the daily weariness of acedia," writes Rebecca Konyndyk DeYoung in *Glittering Vices*, "is steady commitment and daily discipline, even when we don't feel like it."[3] Everything that really matters in life, in other words, requires regular watering— whether or not the mood suits. What's required is practice, the disciplined sport of the tortoise, not the hare. Practice is never once and done. Practice doesn't pull up to a destination, doesn't break the tape and then collapse. Practice drives in circles. It recapitulates, rehearses, repeats.

Practice is about neural pathways and muscle memory. It makes me think of my friend Mabel who, growing up in

China, first learned to play Ping-Pong without a ball. Her coach instructed her to transfer her weight from back foot to front foot while mastering the angle at which she swung the paddle and made imaginary contact. Even after her coach gave her permission to play with a ball, Mabel kept swinging at home, fine-tuning her movement.

That's practice. It's repetitive and often boring, and its benefits, slow and hard-won, can be invisible to the naked eye.

The case of E. P. Pauly, as described in Charles Duhigg's *The Power of Habit*, proved that habit, which is to say practice, is a means for learning, even for a man who had lost all capacity for short-term memory. On the day Pauly walked out the front door of his house and went missing, after the doctors had warned his wife he would never master basic directions, Pauly managed to get himself home without help. After his illness and hospitalization, he had re-learned his neighborhood streets because he had so much practice walking them with his wife.

In his book *After You Believe*, N. T. Wright describes virtue as the product of practice:

> Virtue, in this strict sense, is what happens when someone has made a thousand small choices, requiring effort and concentration, to do something which is good and right but which doesn't "come naturally"—and then, on the thousand and first time, when it really matters, they find that they do what's required "automatically," as we say.[4]

In short, we become what we practice.

Our family might have heeded the warning earlier, before we took to binge-watching all eight seasons of *Brooklyn 99*.

Practicing the Love of God

"Lord of all pots and pans and things . . . make me a saint by getting meals and washing up the plates!" If ever there is a monk to read during the pandemic, it is Brother Lawrence, who served as a kitchen hand in a seventeenth-century French monastery. Pots and pans are quarantine life—and I am measuring the days not simply in small kitchen appliances but in dishwasher cycles.

The best thing I do, by April 2020, is commission my young son Andrew to perform this chore twice daily. Most days he's dutiful and diligent. But sometimes I'll find him, nose buried in a book, scowling in the corner of the family room. "You're learning something about faithfulness," I tell him when a storm brews on his face. "Faithfulness is built on the ordinary things we do faithfully every day." At twelve, he has begun learning the daily drudgeries of holy kingdom life.

Brother Lawrence's religious meditations come to us mostly through the efforts of a man named M. Beaufort, who sought spiritual direction from Brother Lawrence. Brother Lawrence lived in times like ours—plague, political unrest, division in the church—and his frailties were all too human. He faced poverty. He lacked education. From a war injury, he suffered chronic pain and likely lived crip time, this time of bodies rather than clocks.

Brother Lawrence described himself as an awkward man who "broke everything." When he entered the monastery it was as a lay monk, lacking the literacy in Latin required for the priesthood. But despite his commonness and clumsiness, Brother Lawrence's spiritual wisdom gained him renown. It brought men like Beaufort to his kitchen to learn from him.

Those conversations, along with some of the monk's letters, were published in what's now considered a spiritual classic, *The Practice of the Presence of God*. In that text, Brother Lawrence explains how love might be directed to God at any time of day, whether or not it is the fixed hour for prayer:

> The time of business does not with me differ from the time of prayer; and in the noise and clatter of my kitchen, while several persons are at the same time calling for different things, I possess God in as great tranquility as if I were upon my knees at the Blessed Sacrament.[5]

The urgency of time for Brother Lawrence was simple and singular: to inhabit God's nearness.

"We give ourselves a world of trouble," the monk writes,

> and pursue a multitude of practices to attain to a sense of the presence of God. And yet it is so simple. How very much shorter it is and easier to do our common business purely for the love of God, to set His consecrating mark on all we lay hands to, and thereby to foster the sense of His abiding presence by communion of our heart with His![6]

Brother Lawrence is commending the habit of *abiding*, which Jesus commanded on the eve of his arrest, betrayal, and death, recorded in John 15. *Abide in me,* Jesus tells us. *Let my words abide in you. Abide—rest, remain, endure, persevere—in my love.*

To abide is to practice an important paradox: while God's love is fixed and constant, we are not. We return, again and again, as a matter of practice, to a God in whom we "live and move and have our being."[7]

The time management industry, for all its many faults, has understood the importance of practice: of regular, routine, even strenuous effort.[8] But abiding, while a practice, is not a habit of time management. It is not a discrete to-do we check off in the morning before moving on to other tasks. It is not even a habit of mindfulness meant to ward off anxiety and ensure better work performance.

As Brother Lawrence has conceived of it, time is not to be parceled and apportioned—some hours given to God, the rest belonging to us. In fact, *time* may not be the most precise word to describe the resource in question here, in the practice of the presence of God. What is better suggested than time is the faculty of *attention.*

We cannot multiply our minutes, but attention can be ours to devote, to discipline, and to direct.

Of course this devotion, this discipline, this purposeful direction are not easy practices to come by in what people are calling our "attentional economy." According to Matthew Crawford, author of *The World beyond Your Head,* everyone is competing for this resource that "determines what is real for us."[9] Attention is more valuable than time because, unlike time, it can be harnessed. As social media executives understand well, attention can even be sold.

I like to think of the practice of attention according to a description by a little girl who attended one of Kathleen Norris's writing classes in a small town in North Dakota. The class was brainstorming fresh ways to describe the quality of silence.

"Silence," this little girl wrote, "reminds me to take my soul with me wherever I go."[10]

Maybe it's best to say it this way: attention is an unhurried practice, a practice that informs the quality of time. Maybe we could even reconsider the great commandments in a slanted shaft of afternoon light: to love God with all our heart, soul, mind, and strength and to love our neighbor as ourselves is to *attend* them. To notice, to name.

Brother Lawrence tells M. Beaufort, in one of their conversations, about the moment of his conversion, at eighteen, when he *attended* a wintering tree: "Considering that within a little time the leaves would be renewed, and after that the flowers and fruit appear, he received a high view of the providence and power of God, which has never since been effaced from his soul."[11] That naked tree, he says, cut him loose from the love of the world and kindled in him a love for God. It gave him reason for devoting all his attention to the one with power to make him new.

"Let what may come of it, however many be the days remaining to me," the clumsy monk says, up to his elbows in suds. "I will do all things for the love of God."[12]

On Making—and Bending—Rules

I have long been preoccupied with the idea of crafting a "rule of life." For the love of God, yes—and because I like rules. For me, at least, rules lend a sense of security, a sense of sure-footedness. Much like a family household, monasteries are, of course, run by rules, the days not left rudderless but regulated. There are prescribed times for prayer, for work, for meals, for study, for corporate worship. In fact, monastic rules would count, in Matthew Crawford's estimation, as the kind of "jig" that structures our attention and, in limiting our freedom, relieves us of the burden of constantly deciding what might be decided once. Rules can regulate practice, just as practice can regulate spiritual formation.

Margaret Guenther, author of *At Home in the World*, reminds us that "consciously or unconsciously, we all follow a rule."[13] We have routine ways for ordering our daily, monthly, yearly calendars. Our "rules" may serve our desires well—and they may not. They may provide our intentional support, or "trellis," for doing all things for the love of God. Or they may promote self-focus, ingratitude, and acedia, that "laziness of spirit in which the muscles of intention of discernment and boundary have atrophied."[14]

I begin reading about Saint Benedict after the world shuts down because the days have a monastic quality to them. The crisis is an experience of confinement, with the noise and vibration of the world muted and stilled, the seven of us shut in the house. Eventually, I shift from reading *about* Saint Benedict to reading *The Rule of Saint Benedict* itself, slowly and meditatively, over the course of many weeks. It becomes a practice of lectio divina, this attentive reading indifferent to pace.

As I discover, practice is the mode of Benedict's rule. He does not think that love of God or love of neighbor can be downloaded like a zip file. He assumes training will be involved in transferring knowledge into desire:

> All that he once performed with dread, he will now begin to observe without effort, as though naturally, from habit, no longer out of fear of hell, but out of love for Christ, good habit and delight in virtue.[15]

Benedict's rule has to do with the life patterning necessary for the purpose of spiritual transformation.

My initial interest in crafting my own rule of life—this monastic method for planning how to steward the resources of time and money, body and possessions—had mostly to do with misguided reasons of time management. I wanted to achieve the elusive "balance" so many talk about, and I imagined I could somehow plan a life where everything was rightly proportioned: work, family, service, leisure. A rule of life, I mistakenly hoped, would prevent me from disappointing people.

The Rule of Saint Benedict is the most enduring example of a monastic rule regulating the daily, weekly, monthly, and yearly practices of the community for the love of God. Every day, the monks pray at seven prescribed times: lauds, prime, terce, sext, none, vespers, and compline. Allowance is made for the shortness of summer nights, and some of the Bible readings are abbreviated between Easter and the first of November. "From holy Easter to Pentecost, the brothers eat at noon and take supper in the evening. Beginning with Pentecost and continuing throughout the summer, the monks fast until midafternoon on Wednesday and Friday, unless they are working the fields, or the summer heat is oppressive."[16]

This enforced regularity—in time—could seem excessive, but the point is not punctuality, as we think of it.

> Monks were not expected to be punctual; they were expected to be *faithful*. . . . Punctuality relates simply to routine and order; one is punctual because the system requires one to be. Faithfulness relates to one's desire to please God through one's routine practices of worship.[17]

The assumption of Benedict's rule is that Christ's followers are like tradespeople in God's workshop or students in God's school. The rule assumes it will take time to learn to love God and regular practice will be required for competency, as if worship were like a handcraft or a field of academic study. Like knitting or welding. Like geometric proofs or verb conjugation.

This is Simone Weil's important insight in *Waiting on God*, this woman whose own faith grew out of regular practices: first by repeating the words of a seventeenth-century poem by Christian poet George Herbert—"Without my knowing it the recitation had the virtue of a prayer"—then by regular repetition of the Lord's Prayer, which she interrupted whenever her attention wandered. "The effect of this practice is extraordinary and surprises me every time, for, although I experience it each day, it exceeds my expectations at each repetition."[18]

In one of Weil's essays, she draws comparison to the effort one might make, bent over a page of math problems, to the efforts in the spiritual life. Whether or not one ever solves for x, the muscle of attention has been worked and strengthened. Sin, according to Weil, is a misapplication of attention, a "turning of our gaze in the wrong direction."[19]

At the beach, at the beginning of March 2020, on the precipice of the world's imminent collapse, I took pages of college-ruled paper to start working on my "rule." At the top of the first page, I copied Psalm 119:5: "Oh that my ways may be steadfast in keeping your statutes!" Steadfastness was the weight I was looking for, the anchor I lacked. I didn't want to be such a spiritual dilettante.

I started by listing questions to discuss with Ryan later that week. What should be our family rhythms for vacationing? For seeing our families in the States? For getting away together as a couple? What should be our weekly hospitality rhythms, given his introversion and my often unrealistic energies? Did our volunteer commitments at church need to be reevaluated and pared down? What did our children need from us, given that they were, one by one, leaving the nest? What friendships mattered most? The point of this "rule" exercise wasn't time and its management, although time was a consideration. The point was the practice of conversion, this continual process of turning my feet to God's ways.

I started to make daily practice goals: *One hour—Scripture reading, journaling, prayer, other reading.* Then I started to make weekly practice goals: *Sabbath—no shopping, no laundry, no paid work.* I set down some limits on the time I would spend traveling each month for work, and I planned for one day a month to pray, review the calendar, and fast.

My rule remains a work in progress. And that's the beauty of practice.

In his conversations with M. Beaufort, Brother Lawrence says that practicing the presence of God takes, well, practice.

> In order to form a habit of conversing with God continually, and referring all we do to Him, we must first apply to Him with some diligence; but that after little care we should find his love inwardly excite us to it without any difficulty.[20]

Diligence, as a modifier of practice, makes me think of the four-octave piano scales I played every day for years as a child. The arpeggios. The Hanon exercises. Practice time was what I recorded in the flimsy black notebook my teacher opened every week, looking through the reading glasses perched on her nose that otherwise hung from a chain around her neck.

Practice was tedious, and sometimes I fudged the minutes. To be sure, sometimes I bent the *rules*.

Your Time to Shine

The spiritual life has more to do with habits than epiphanies. I try remembering this on the third day of Advent, when we've not had time to put up our Christmas tree or buy candles for the Advent wreath. "Does the shepherds' candle come first?" Andrew asks, a question I can't answer despite having read the same little blue devotional book every year at Advent since his older sister, Audrey, was small.

Fleming Rutledge has written that Advent begins in the dark, and this feels especially true this year, as I am just home from a visit with my friend Heather who, six months ago, was diagnosed with metastic breast cancer. I am tired. I am behind on life. I want to *feel* God's nearness, but habits are the only solid ground beneath my feet.

Habits tell the story of the nation of Israel, bound by their weekly observance of Sabbath, their Kosher practices, their annual feasts and pilgrimages, their daily recitations of the Shema. *Hear, O Israel, the Lord our God, the Lord is one.* Habits tell the story of Jesus: how he regularly escaped alone for prayer in the morning; how he regularly participated in synagogue worship; how he, the tree of Psalm 1, meditated on Scripture day and night.

Habits tell the story of the early church, who committed themselves not only to the teachings of Scripture but also to learning from "training manuals" like the Didache, a text short enough to be memorized. The Didache was a wisdom text, and it called Christians to choose between two ways: the way of life or the way of death. The Didache didn't simply enforce a system of theological ideas to learn but insisted "that these themes must be embodied and practiced."[21] The Didache called for habits of hospitality, ministry to the poor, regular fasting, daily gatherings with other believers, and reconciling conflict, and it gave instructions for discerning between false and true prophets. "Every prophet who teaches the truth but fails to practice what he preaches is a false prophet."[22]

I open my prayer book this third morning of Advent as soon as I sit down to my desk. This exercise of fixed-hour prayer is a way to practice the Christian life, if not always to feel God's nearness. Many days, I come to the practice almost against my will. Many other days, I race through it perfunctorily. Still, I say the words of the prayer Jesus taught his disciples to pray—even if, unlike with Weil, Christ doesn't come down and take immediate possession of me, as she described of her own experience.

I keep going. I repeat the words of the prayer appointed for the week, this prayer that will routinely be on my lips every morning, every midday, and every evening when I don't forget: *Almighty God, give us all grace to cast away the works of darkness, and put on the armor of light, now in the time of this mortal life in which your Son Jesus Christ came to visit us in great humility.*[23] I don't wait for the mood to strike to pray. Prayer brings me back to God, wandering and wild dog that I am.

It's interesting how important the word *practice* is in the lexicon of the New Testament. When the apostle Paul wrote to his young disciple Timothy, he told him to train in godliness, to "practice" these things . . . so that all may see his progress. When Paul closed his letter to the Philippians, he wrote, "What you have learned and received and heard and seen in me—practice these things, and the God of peace will be with you."[24] When the writer of Hebrews talked about the spiritual capacity for discernment, he said it was formed by practice, the practice of distinguishing good from evil. Practice is not always the moralism we often think it is; it is a feature of regular obedience to Jesus, of this race we train for and run to win.

And practice isn't just a New Testament idea. It's fundamental to the formation of wisdom, which we see pictured in Psalm 1: "Blessed is the man who walks not in the counsel of the wicked, nor stands in the way of sinners, nor sits in the seat of scoffers; but his delight is in the law of the LORD, and on his law he meditates day and night."[25] To regularly take in the story of Scripture and rehearse the goodness, faithfulness, and power of God is a practice that roots us deeply and secures us in storm. It's why early church father Tertullian said Christians aren't born, they're made. It's why the late Dallas Willard wrote that Christians must learn to train, not try. The paradox of transformation is that while it's a work God does in us, it's also a work we cooperate with, even participate in. It's both gift and effort, rest and work.

Grace and Practice

The Bible's wisdom tradition makes clear that wisdom is something learned and practiced first at home, as children hear and heed the instruction of their parents. Wisdom is not secret and hidden knowledge; it is transferred from generation to generation. And wisdom is not received ready-made but forged in the furnace of everyday affairs. As one scholar writes about the woman praised in Proverbs 31, "Here are the disciplined qualities and habits that make for stability and that work with the grain of God's world."[26]

In his commentary on Proverbs, Derek Kidner notes that one synonym for wisdom, *instruction* (or *training*), gives "notice at once that wisdom will be hard-won, a quality of character as much as of mind."[27] "Wisdom is not to be had through extra-mural study," Kidner explains. "It is for disciples only." And what's required for these disciples, according to the book of Proverbs, is devotion, attention. *Fear of the Lord.* "Wisdom is for the humbly eager."[28] It is not for the sluggard, the fool, the scoffer. It is for those who know enough to know what they don't know, who submit themselves to the training required to gain what they lack.

It is for those who *practice*—which is something I failed to do leading up to a family tennis match, a couple of years ago. Ryan was paired with Andrew, and I with Colin. It's not hard to imagine Colin, the more intensely competitive of the two, and his disappointment when I missed volley after volley at the net. "That was your time to shine," he told me again and again, exasperated.

"How can I shine when I never practice?"

It wasn't an excuse he accepted, by the way.

Two Steps Forward

I don't know exactly when I start leaving my phone upstairs in the morning, after I turn my alarm off. But before I know it, this becomes a habit, a daily, intentional practice. My eyes flutter open, and I reach for my phone to silence the buzzing. Then I leave it there, like a cold fish I've refused to touch. I don't check messages, don't quickly scan email or the day's headlines.

The world might be shattering around me or planes might be falling from the sky, but I don't yet know what to be angry about or grieve. The rest of the day, I'll fight feeling hostage to my phone. But for now, I muzzle it. Tell it to stand down. I shuffle downstairs in my slippers, make a cup of coffee, and settle into my chair. For the first hours of the day, I live inside the soundless cocoon of my house, oblivious to all other noise except, perhaps, the garbage truck rumbling down the street by 7:00 a.m.

Weil says God rewards the soul that thinks of him with

attention and love. *Maybe*. And maybe this is just good practice.

When a revival swept across Wales in the early twentieth century, the leaders of that movement, traveling from village to village preaching the gospel, routinely asked people not simply to put away unconfessed sin but also to forsake "doubtful habits."[29] I wonder, of course, about those acts of repentance. To think these were people living without smartphones. To think they lived entire hours, entire days within the narrow confines of embodied rather than mediated experience. It is easy to envy the simpler conditions of their lives.

Distraction is not a modern phenomenon. We are endlessly inventive about ways to avoid attending God and neighbor. Still, it certainly seems true that God's got more competition these days. Distraction is a major obstacle to forming better habits in time. This is to say nothing of the zeitgeist of acedia, this mood of listlessness inspired by the technological environment. Effort has become our greatest enemy—ease our greatest desire. If I can't be bothered to get up from the couch to turn out the light, barking orders to Alexa instead, how will I rally the energies required for transformation?

Who do I become when I can't bother practicing?

"Those with acedia are slothful," writes Rebecca Konyndyk DeYoung.

> They want an easy spiritual life. They find detachment from their old selfish nature too difficult, painful, and burdensome, so they neglect to perform the actions that would maintain and deepen relationships of love.[30]

I'm starting to think our phones should come with warning labels, in all caps: BEWARE THE DANGERS OF THIS PRACTICE.

I can't help but think of Wormwood's advice to his nephew, the senior devil teaching his young apprentice the art of temptation. He instructed him to distract his subject from considering his most obvious daily routines, having him focus instead on more esoteric preoccupations.[31] Wormwood knew there was little harm in allowing Christians to indulge the *moods* of the faithful life. What must be prevented instead was attention toward everyday habits. *Never let Christians think of holiness as practice.*

It is rare that any of my children compliment me. This is not surprising, of course. Mothers are for admiring when they're eulogized. Routinely, I am told by my many children of my shortcomings: things I can and should fix, like the dinner menu; things I cannot, like the size of my nose. It's why I've never forgotten when one of my daughters said, with a hint of begrudging praise, that I was so "moderate." She was thinking less of my political persuasions and more my avoidance of extremes.

On the one hand, "moderate" makes me think of wool cardigans, smart shoes, and mousy brown hair. "Moderate" is not a hallowed virtue on Instagram or TikTok or Twitter. On the other hand, "moderate" makes me think of Benedict's rule, this careful oversight of possessions and food and time and speech. It makes me think of the zeal we temper and train through practice, even rules.

Maybe I am making progress after all.

TO CONSIDER

What "rules" are you now practicing with regard to work, family, friendship, leisure, and God?

Are your habits reinforcing what you most deeply value? How are they running counter to the values of God's kingdom?

What doubtful habits can you identify in your life? What doubtful digital habits?

Through what means is God calling you to practice your way, by his grace, into faithfulness and love?

TO PRAY

God, I confess I am often divided against myself. I want to consent to your good work in me, but I also resist the effort I must contribute along the way. I'm often too distracted to engage the practices necessary for attending you with all my heart, all my soul, all my mind, all my strength. I'm often too lazy to attend my neighbor as myself. Work in me the will to work out my salvation with fear and trembling in routine, ordinary, daily practices.

Enjoy

As we take up burdens, even as we walk through the valley of the shadow of death, we find the fullness of God's own joy.

Heather and I were twenty-four when we became friends. *I hope she isn't perky and petite,* Heather said to herself after I called to invite her and her husband, Dave, to a small group we were leading at our church. Fortunately, she forgave me these and other faults, including my clumsy leadership of that group that became our first fight.

My friendship with Heather is like many friendships I've made in my peripatetic life. After we both moved away from Chicago, our friendship has been sustained with very occasional visits and long phone calls. It abides long periods of silence where neither of us wonders if the other is dead or angry, where we grant that work and parenting and changing furnace filters have kept us busy and preoccupied. We brought our first babies into the world together, which counts for a lot in the life span of friendship.

But on May 6, 2021, I learn that my friend Heather might be dead soon, or at least much sooner than either of us would have thought possible. "As some of you know," she writes, "I've had increasingly debilitating back pain over the past few months." She had an MRI and received life-altering results: "Secondary cancer in my spine." She includes a picture of herself standing in front of her fireplace, dressed in a yellow cardigan embroidered with small pink flowers, black pants, and a pair of yellow Converse high-tops. The picture—of seeming health—is taken from the shoulders down, so I don't know whether Heather is feebly smiling or grimacing to share this catastrophic news.

I take the news terribly. The borders between Canada and the United Kingdom, where Heather lives, are closed, and even if I did attempt to travel on the pretext of mortal urgency, I would face a ten-day quarantine in Scotland upon my arrival and a fourteen-day quarantine in Toronto upon my return. The only thing I can do, when I learn that my long-standing, nearly lifelong friend has incurable cancer, is buy my own pair of yellow Converse high-tops and wear them as I circle my block praying for her, her husband, and their two teenage boys.

After that first email to friends, Heather began writing a blog, *The Incurable*, on Substack.[1] Reading her posts nearly every week, I've been struck by how often she writes of joy. Whatever joy means, it is not what most people write about, not when your bones are riddled with cancer and you can no longer take a single step unassisted. Joy does not seem to be the key to making sense of this new housebound life of yours, with crutches, walker, and wheelchair crowding your living room. You don't expect joy to greet you the day you come home with news of life-threatening disease. But as the New Testament writer James suggests, when he writes about meeting trials of many kinds, Heather is somehow *counting it joy* after tumors have caused the collapse of her T5 vertebra and compression in her spinal cord.

"Here is where I start to run out of words to describe all of the love and support and encouragement and prayers that have been poured over us," she writes in her second blog post, "The Paradox of Pain." "I have felt love-bombed in the best possible ways as you marvelous, delightful people have showered me with your gifts," she tells friends receiving her words.[2]

In subsequent posts, Heather says she will not "sugar-coat" the situation, especially when her oncologist takes an early retirement and there is no one in all of *bonnie Fife* to read her latest scans. But she does decide for joy, even calls it a "discipline," this practice of choosing to praise the God from whom she is receiving each day as gift. She even writes of her decision to continue wearing her #blessed necklace, not because her diagnosis is the blessing—"Healing is a gift; cancer is not"—but because she is a child of God, comforted by his merciful presence.

Six months after her diagnosis, she celebrates: "I'm still here."

Everything is not perfect—nor will it be. All our questions are not answered—nor are they likely to be. But joy does not depend on perfection or knowledge. Sometimes joy is the appreciation of sitting with the person you love on your falling-apart couch while you watch fireworks, and the awareness that you had no guarantee of this moment six months ago but you are so thankful to be here for it.[3]

I think of Heather and her family when my fixed-hour prayer book reminds me to pray for those who sow with tears, then reap with songs of joy. Those who go out weeping, *carrying the seed*, who will come again with joy, shouldering their sheaves.[4]

The Paradox of Joy

The Bible speaks of joy as full of paradox. We see this in the time preoccupied psalm attributed to Moses, where he asks to learn to number his days in order to gain a heart of wisdom: "Make us glad for as many days as you have afflicted us, and for as many years as we have seen evil," he writes. "The years of our life are seventy, or even by reason of strength eighty; yet their span is but toil and trouble."[5] Moses imagined time and its troubles surrendered—somehow—to joy's practice of gladness.

Moses lived a lifetime of plagues: ten plagues that swept the nation out of the Egyptian furnace of slavery, followed by wilderness plagues God sent to discipline his stubborn children in their forty years of wandering. Moses was never spared the trouble of this fallen life, and he was even denied his own final request to see the promised land. And still, Moses somehow thought it possible to experience, at some deep level, a deep and abiding joy. "Satisfy us in the morning with your steadfast love, that we may rejoice and be glad all our days."[6]

Moses knew that joy eddies with grief in this muddy river called time. He knew that joy, even in the valley of the shadow of death, can be a constant. Even there, with the specter of doom as thick as London fog, God is with us, holding us fast.

In the shadow of COVID, it has been difficult to experience joy, even for those of us who know God's constancy and try to practice his nearness. In Toronto, gyms, salons, movie theatres, museums, schools, and churches were closed during our long lockdown—some for more than a year.

When you can't leave the house, where do you find joy?

"At least we won't be alone this Christmas," I say to Ryan as the two of us limp through our second pandemic November. The days are getting shorter and darker, but the neighborhood twinkles with color. And the neighbors half a block down have put out their blow-up Buddy the Elf in their front yard, the one with his mouth agape. SANTAAAAA!

In these trying days, we have begun to see that joy has the shape of a found poem—"bits and bobs," as my friend Heather would say, repeating the British colloquialism. Joy isn't always unearthed whole; it can be collected in collage, scavenged like copper pennies.[7] Joy requires its own stubborn habits of attention.

Joy, in the Bible, is less mood and more imperative: "Rejoice in the Lord always," the apostle Paul writes from a cramped prison cell. "Again I will say, rejoice."[8] In the

Wycliffite English translation of the Bible, we see this quality of joy's decision in its rendering of Luke 1:14, where the angel announces to Zechariah that his wife will give birth to a son. "And many should *enjoy* in his nativity."[9]

In hindsight, our isolated Christmas 2020 season was not disastrous. We were not able to visit family or receive guests, but we started new family traditions, including changing into our pajamas early every Sunday night, piling into the car after dinner, and driving around Toronto to see Christmas lights. We recorded our first audio version of Charles Dickens's *A Christmas Carol* and discovered Nathan's talent for voice acting. *In life, I was your partner, Jaaacob Marley.* We entered our church's Zoom gingerbread house contest—and made sure to devastate our opponents with a carefully engineered replica of our own house, complete with a garage and pretzeled herringbone front walk. And, of course, we watched our favorite Christmas movies as well as a couple of new ones, including one I'd seen enthusiastically recommended on social media.

"Who said this was good?" the kids asked when we finally shut off a new Netflix original two-thirds of the way through. We yanked out our phones to find an honest review, which we knew we'd found when, in the title, the review said the movie made Christmas feel "exhausting."

"There is not one scene in [this no good, very bad film] where one wonders, even just for a moment, if things will turn out alright," the reviewer said.[10] The movie had parodied joy, had turned it—as we often do—into something entirely uncomplicated.

Joy to the World

Confusion reigns about the difference between joy and happiness and this state of being "blessed." Is joy more spiritual than happiness? Is #blessed a caption best reserved for social media posts after you've returned from the beach, sun-kissed and smiling? Whatever the differences, surely these words signal where all of time's aspirations travel. Yes, we want to get things done, but mostly we want life to taste as sweet as a summer peach. We want to drink its nectar, let its sticky juice drip and dry on our chins.

This search for joy is implied in the search for wisdom, according to the psalmist: "Come, O children, listen to me; I will teach you the fear of the LORD. What man is there who desires life and loves many days, that he may see good? Keep your tongue from evil and your lips from speaking deceit."[11] Joy is at the heart of the Bible's framing of wisdom: to be wise is to live life well.

Most importantly, joy is at the heart of the gospel: to follow Jesus is to find his fullness of joy.

Joy can be otherworldly, yes—and it also has something to do with the birthdays Esther, Jill, and I celebrate together during our pandemic year: decadent meringue desserts and fizzy flutes of champagne in the middle of the afternoon. These are women with whom I sit outside under twinkle lights, bundled up against all kinds of weather, because of restrictions on indoor gatherings. I find so much unabated joy in these friendships—because joy likes company.

Maybe I can also talk about finding joy when my twin sons and I head to the beach on a day about a month before

Lake Ontario is fully frozen. The sky is gray and unyielding, the wind is blustery, and Colin and Andrew collect sticks to throw to our three-year-old goldendoodle, Via. The sticks land in the shallows, and though Via paws at the water's edge, watching the sticks float and watching other dogs paddle away from her as if begging her to follow, she clambers back onto the rocks without attempting to retrieve them. "Let's go to the beach again!" Colin begs every day for a week. He knows there is joy in the natural world at its most wintry and wild, joy because "the heavens declare the glory of God, and the sky above proclaims his handiwork."[12]

Or maybe I could say that joy is something to find beneath the soaring ceiling of my church's 1876 sanctuary in downtown Toronto, the sun filtering through the opalescent stained-glass Trinity windows (more recently installed in 1989): the Father on the north side, represented in the red of the dawn; the Son on the south side, represented in the blue of baptism; the Spirit on the west side, represented by the yellow of blessing. The psalmist knew the joy of God's people gathered to enjoy God's presence: "For a day in your courts is better than a thousand elsewhere."[13]

What I am trying to do is avoid sanctimony, the parading, affected sort of holiness that pretends a disinterest in the world as if that were automatically interest in God. Joy, especially as it's figured in the Old Testament prophets, is as leggy as good wine, as golden as summer grain. Joy, in the Old Testament, pours green and pungent, like a good olive oil. When Jeremiah promises that God will return his people to their land, after their exile for sin is ended, he describes that return like this:

They shall come and sing aloud on the height of
    Zion,
  and they shall be radiant over the goodness of
    the LORD,
over the grain, the wine, and the oil,
  and over the young of the flock and the herd;
their life shall be like a watered garden,
  and they shall languish no more.
Then shall the young women rejoice in the dance,
  and the young men and the old shall be merry.
I will turn their mourning into joy;
  I will comfort them, and give them gladness for
    sorrow.[14]

"It has seemed to me sometimes as though the Lord breathes on this poor gray ember of Creation and it turns to radiance," John Ames, a rural pastor, writes in one of his final letters to his son.[15] Ames is the protagonist of the epistolary novel *Gilead*, and his health is failing. He is leaving his wife, his young son, and this world he has come to love and doesn't apologize for loving. "There are a thousand thousand reasons to live this life, every one of them sufficient," Ames writes.[16]

To feel joy—at the first purple crocus to break ground in the spring, at a horse's lips stealing apple pieces from your hand, at a sunset over Lake Huron with the horizon line beribboned in orange—is to lose sense of other urgencies. To experience joy—as a night singing karaoke with your teenagers in some downtown dive, as a live performance of Arturo Márquez's Danzón No. 2 with your daughter playing the clarinet solos—is to find your own typically fragmented presence re-collected. Joy can find you through the fissures of ordinary life, bubbling up like a hidden spring—and it can remind you there will be a day when the veil is torn from this world and we will all greet the Christ as John the Baptist did in utero. "When the sound of your greeting came to my ears, the baby in my womb leaped for joy," his mother told the mother of Jesus.[17]

To put it more surprisingly, joy is the thing parodied at the slot machine: when time falls away and you've been standing there eight, twelve hours without consciousness of the turning, tilting world. Natasha Dow Schüll has extensively researched the world of compulsive gambling, and she understands that "players are seeking an intoxicating experience in the moment—an experience outside of time . . . in which the pressures and contingencies of life are suspended."[18] It's joy, or the manufactured semblance of it, that has power to jam the gears of the clock. It's joy that lures us into *kairos* time, this time kept in eternity. C. S. Lewis wondered if all pleasures weren't substitutes for joy.[19]

I am not holding up compulsive gamblers as models for imitation in the habit of joy. Schüll's research also found that it is not uncommon for compulsive gamblers to stand long enough to develop blood clots or go into cardiac arrest. Paramedics dread calls from Vegas casinos because other players "won't get out of the way to let the paramedics do their jobs; they won't leave their machines." One woman Schüll interviewed confessed that she wore dark colors "so it won't show when she urinates on herself."[20] It doesn't seem too far of a stretch to say that human beings don't always know how to choose the best sources of joy.

In the garden of Eden, God's first directives were the commands to work, to worship, and to enjoy. *Be fruitful and multiply. Everything you need, I have given. Live long in this land. Send your roots deep into the groundwater of my sustaining love. Feast here, in this home I have prepared for you.*

In the garden, joy never had to be justified.

Of course, this primordial joy was jeopardized the moment it was plucked from a tree and taken on its own terms. "I'll have my gift, thank you very much," our human parents said, cutting themselves off from God, from the garden, and even from the tree whose fruit had the power to give them life. Christians call this desire for autonomous joy—joy apart from God and apart from submission to God's will—*sin*. And sin provides a way to understand the failing modern project, this self-determined, self-empowered, self-congratulating, even self-blaming enterprise of making your best life now. We are a deeply unhappy people because, for joy to be our reward today, it will also have to be our sole responsibility.

The phenomenon of rising rates of anxiety and depression can be located, among other places, at the intense pressures we've put ourselves under to make an Instagram-worthy life. "Any quick perusal of the self-help section of a bookstore," writes Matthew Crawford,

> teaches that the central character in our contemporary drama is a being who must choose what he is to be and bring about his transformation through an effort of the will. It is a heroic project of open-ended, ultimately groundless self-making.[21]

Self-help is an industry that enthrones the self, and though this can at times feel empowering, it's ultimately defeating. Your problems are always yours to solve through your efforts and cunning and self-discipline.

Self-improvement is an exhausting, thriving business.

Time management is just one version of the self-help industry, and its promise—of eliminating stress from your life—is ultimately a promise about joy. "Take heart," writes David Allen in an early chapter of *Getting Things Done*. He describes setting up essential systems for "workflow mastery"—systems that involve outfitting an office, choosing an analog or digital organizer for task lists, and creating a personal reference file. Allen's detail is granular—and his promise is bold. "I've seen people go from resisting to actually enjoying sorting through their piles and digital world once their personal filing system is set up and humming."[22]

Just yesterday, I looked at the website for a popular time management system trying to sell me on a consumer vision that will "banish distractions," "tame [my] to-do list," and "achieve big goals." These are synonyms for time management joy. "You sink into bed exhausted, but nothing feels done," the marketing copy describes of my problem. I can't help but remember my blurry three pages, at 9:30 p.m., and the few moments before my eyes drooped shut, my book abandoned on my nightstand. "The daily whirlwind of activities swept you away while your greatest priorities took a back seat." I think of the half hour I spent that day wringing water from the sweaters I hand-washed. "We believe neverending to-do lists are the source of overwhelm and disappointment in life. You don't have to let your to-do list call the shots. There's a better way."[23] You can have joy if, for $39.99, you BUY NOW.

The Good Life

After we arrive in Vancouver, I am sleepless for two nights. I am not enjoying myself. I feel guilty that we left Toronto three days after another lockdown. But some of my unease burns off with the fog on the morning we arrive at the base of a small mountain at the edge of Squamish. When we meet our guide, James, he is unpacking large duffel bags from his beat-up van. The sun is not yet overhead, and Camille and Colin are shivering in their thin sweatshirts.

James gives us all the necessary instructions to climb and to belay, and the tutorial goes by so quickly I'm worried I won't have it mastered. It surprises me, then, how easily we put our lives into each other's hands: clipping, knotting, looping, tugging. We don orange helmets and take turns scrambling up the face of the rock.

On one pass that requires we jam our hands along a dark, spidery crevice, I make it sixty feet up—then bail when the last twenty feet require shimmying up what looks like smooth, sheer glass. Camille is at the belay. I look down, and she has both hands securely on the rope. Before I tell her I am "ready to lower," I lean against the mountain and take in the view. Western hemlock. Western red cedar. Douglas fir. Trees made tall and strong with time. I let my face warm against the rock and feel happy and #blessed and full of sudden joy.

Vacation has, of course, become the stand-in for the good life. We seek to *enjoy* time by throwing off mundanity. We travel in search of joy. And it's true there is something to vacation—its new views, its unhurried time—that is inherently enjoyable. On vacation, you don't normally do the laundry or the dishes. You sleep late. You ignore email. You forget you're a human being with a cable bill and rent. Vacation is the idyll of life at its most carefree, most careless. Joy greets you there barefoot, looking the slouchy part of Matthew McConaughey behind the wheel of his Lincoln.

I'm not down on vacations. No, we've needed escapes from the pandemic grind, and we've taken them. But escape is not the regular mode of the joyful life. Paradoxically, burdens are. One measure of Christian joy is its capacity for pushing its wild, stubborn head through the cracks of quotidian life. One test of joy is its ability to withstand acedia's withering noonday sun.

My friend Christina Crook writes about this in her second book, *Good Burdens*, where she seeks to reimagine how to "live joyfully in a digital age." Christina's lifework is dedicated to exploring the good burdens of making lives that make for joy, these "commitments that tether us to people and the physical world."[24] Although these real-world, embodied commitments challenge our toxic relationships to our devices, she says, it's not simply about breaking up with our smartphone. Rather, she writes, it's about the "reclamation of effortful living."[25]

The tethering commitments Christina describes explain some of what I've depicted in this chapter, between friendship and fizzy champagne, between children and wintry days, between stained-glass windows and church life. Joy isn't escaping my life but entering it more fully: with attention, with gratitude, with commitment to offering myself in all things for the love of God and neighbor. Joy is even willing myself to be interrupted by the freight of life, which Christina reminds me is another meaning of the word *burden*.

Freighted joy involves suffering, of course. This is the meaning of the incarnation. God himself might have stayed an arm's length away from this cosmos, this realm of darkness. God might have exempted himself from the burdens of time—and its attendant burden of death. But he embraced those burdens, knowing full well that the world would reject its own Joy. God walked the neighborhood of the world—and the world did not leap with joy as unborn John the Baptist did. It gnashed its teeth. It crucified him.

Living the Lord's time is always a resistance movement. We will not find joy, as Christina says, in the three sirens of consumerism: comfort, control, and convenience. We will not find it in hot tubs and espresso machines, in fancy grills and fancier vacations. We won't find it in technology's thirsty pursuit of the new. We will find joy tethered to God and his good world. We might even find joy on the very worst of days, when cancer forecloses on the future we'd imagined for ourselves.

The joy of the Lord is just that stubborn, just that steadfast, just that full of surprise.

Another way to speak of joy and its resistance is to borrow from German sociologist Hartmut Rosa.[26] Rosa's work has become important for those interested, as I am, in the ubiquitous experience of time anxiety. Rosa has studied the accelerating pace of modern life but has come to suggest we need more than habits of slowing down as our antidote, especially for those of us privileged enough to have a choice in the matter.

Our greatest problem, according to Rosa, isn't the pace of modern life but rather the experience of alienation that existential speed produces. We don't lack joy simply because we're running too fast. It's that we are hurrying *past* life and the "resonant" encounters we might have with it. The only way we've imagined combatting our time anxiety, then, is by amassing resources for this future we are hurtling toward.

Life on speed isn't just foolishness, says Rosa. It's joylessness. It's like perpetual fall for anxious squirrels. We hide our acorns and hope to remember, after winter's first snow, exactly where in the yard we've buried them. Resistance—to this joyless habit of preparing for life rather than living it—involves resonant experiences of "fuller time." And fuller time always involves us with experience of the other: the world, its guests, God. Maybe this is why vacations, if we're privileged enough to take them, prove to be some of our most resonant time. Less preoccupied with finishing our to-do list, we give ourselves permission to enjoy.

According to Rosa, resonance—this experience of the fullness of time—is organized around two axes: the vertical represents religion, art, nature, history, the transcendence of God; the horizonal axis represents friendship, marriage, family, relationships of love.[27] Given the degree to which we've been severed from many of these sources of joy since March 2020, it's no wonder *languishing* has been our collective experience of time.

I'm not necessarily suggesting we take more vacations, although it's worth noting Americans take less vacation time than their Western counterparts. No, the trick is bringing our souls with us into all of time, believing we can even *enjoy* the burdens of life if we can be fully present to the people and the places they represent. Writes Andrew Root, from whom I learned about Rosa's work,

> We discover that acceleration's gift of speeding us up for the sake of a freedom to be and do whatever we want, in the end, is unveiled (shockingly) as no freedom at all. The closer we get to such "freedom," the more we're alienated from life itself. Rather, we discover life, to draw from Luther, not in being free from others but in the freedom to be with and for those we encounter in attachments of love, friendship, and parenting/family (care).[28]

Searching in the Oxford English Dictionary, I find an alternative meaning for *enjoy*, one that captures this joy of the burdened, tethered, committed life. Whereas we usually imagine *enjoy* as an intransitive verb, in which the subject of the sentence benefits from the action—"I enjoy fizzy flutes of champagne"—another use of *enjoy* is transitive, its action performed upon another. *Enjoy*, in this sense, means "to put into a joyous condition, to make happy, to give pleasure to."[29]

I also find a fifteenth-century example of this form of the verb, which signals how joy can forsake its own ease: "For to gladde and enjoye the people."

Surprised by Joy

I am no expert on St. Ignatius of Loyola, founder of the Jesuits, but almost inadvertently I begin practicing Ignatian examen as I keep pandemic pages in my very sloppy handwriting. I slow down to consider not just the world but how I feel in these singular and strange days. What I am doing, without knowing it, is noticing the occasional stabbings of joy felt in routine days: between unloading the dishwasher in the morning and watching (too much) Netflix at night.

My husband, Ryan, takes up this practice too, when after a season of burnout I give him a copy of *The Monk Manual*, a "daily system for peaceful being and purposeful doing." A planner may not change your life, but as proved true in my husband's case, it can change your practice of it. Guided by the questions in this system focused on gratitude, both of us began asking about the most meaningful moments of our days, about the gifts we noticed ourselves receiving. "When we lead with gratitude," the planner's website explains, "we allow the layers of our fears to slowly peel away, pushing us to be fully present, fully ourselves, and fully alive."[30] To return to Rosa's language, gratitude is a practice of resonance.

Examen holds value for those preoccupied with time—those hoping to number their days in order to gain a heart of wisdom. Examen is the practice of attending not simply to the events and circumstances of our lives but also to our reactions to them. It's more preoccupied with yesterday than tomorrow. We ask ourselves, Where do we find consolation, this "felt increase in faith, hope and love" when we draw near to God? And where do we find desolation, this "troubled spirit" of "anxiety, restlessness, doubts, self-loathing, and dejection"?[31] Examen is the kind of practice that surfaces joy's surprise.

And I'm always surprised by the places where I'm *enjoying* time. Yes, on occasion, it's with my face against the warmed rock of a mountain, the wind whipping through my hair. But often it's there to greet me when, at first, I'm grumbling about bringing groceries to my friend Constance and her three little boys. I know for certain this family figures in the parable Jesus told about sheep and goats and the least of these. But the boys are loud, and I am often forced to park *a whole block* from their apartment.

Still, I go, at least most weeks. When I arrive and after I knock, I hear the clamor of skittering feet, three little boys shrieking my name. Constance opens the door, looking tired, and she and I sit at the small round table by the kitchen. Sometimes she offers me a steaming plate of chicken gizzards, if that's what's simmering on the stove. Always the boys flap around us, like summer moths circling a porch light.

When I leave, the three of them throw their arms around my waist and burrow into me. "You're going?" they ask plaintively. I inhale the clean of their hair, the lotion with which they've been slathered that morning. I remember the days my own children were waist high and wildly affectionate.

Their arms loosen and, looking up at me, they suddenly get bossy. "Next time, bring McDonald's," they bark, while Constance looks on, embarrassed.

"I will," I say. "But you'll have to remember to say thank you."

I turn, closing the door behind me. *Thank you,* I say, marveling how God *enjoys* me.

TO CONSIDER

What are some of your misconceptions about joy?

What would it look like to find joy in your everyday life? In your suffering?

What burdens of life, what "tethering commitments," do you resist that might ultimately prove to be sources of joy?

TO PRAY

Father, I confess I lack wisdom for choosing my joy rightly. I don't remember you are the source of constant, unending joy, and I don't acknowledge that joy is possible in seasons of pain. Help me to learn the joy of obedience, the joy of surrender, the joy of generosity, and when I drink in the many goodnesses of this created world, let it lead me to joyful praise.

Remember

As we count on time as fleeting, we ask God for wisdom to number our days and remember their end.

It is an easy overnight flight from Toronto to London on a Thursday in November. Despite having to wear a mask, I manage to sleep a couple of hours on the plane, one seat—and enough comfortable space—between me and the woman who sleeps with her head resting against the window. I land at Heathrow before 6:00 a.m., and after I am easily through customs, I have enough time to grab coffee at Starbucks while waiting for my connecting flight to Edinburgh. When I ask for cream, the barista looks at me quizzically. "Pouring cream?" she asks. I nod, and soon discover its deliciousness, nearly as thick as molasses.

On this uncharacteristically temperate morning, the Edinburgh taxi driver picks me up in a large van. For the ninety-minute drive to the small fishing village where my friend Heather lives, my new Scottish friend keeps up a chatty narration. Past the Queensferry Crossing, he indicates the Amazon fulfillment center on the left—the largest in the UK.

Ironically, I arrive at Heather's house the same moment as an Amazon delivery person. Together, we climb the stairs and ring the bell, peering through the glass. Heather, gripping her elbow crutch, her two miniature schnauzers circling behind her, opens the door to us both.

To see my friend on this day, wearing lipstick and earrings and having blow-dried her blond hair, is not to believe she is being treated for incurable cancer. "Metastatic spinal cord compression," she tells me a couple of days later, as I reshelve books on the bookcases some of her other friends moved a couple of days ago. Avoiding her eyes, I don't ask her about prognosis. I only know she has warned her mother not to look it up.

In chapter 4 of *The Rule of Saint Benedict*, monks are given instructions about "The Tools for Good Works." Tools are of course required, because in Benedict's fourth-century version of life with God, obedience is "labor" and disobedience "sloth." The monks are reminded to love God, to love their neighbor, to obey the Ten Commandments and the Golden Rule. They are instructed in practices of self-renunciation: "Do not pamper yourself, but love fasting." They are commanded to offer practical service to others: "You must relieve the lot of the poor, clothe the naked, visit the sick, and bury the dead. Go to help the troubled and console the sorrowing."[1] A couple of paragraphs later, monks are soberly reminded of life's brevity on this tilting, turning planet and asked to regularly admit their fate.

"Live in fear of judgment day and have a great horror of hell. Yearn for everlasting life with holy desire. Day by day *remind yourself that you are going to die.*"[2] Death, writes Benedict, will regulate the monks' behavior "hour by hour." They will sense God's gaze upon them, and they will guard their lips, their thoughts. They will even, as necessary, moderate "boisterous laughter."

It seems, at first glance, that Benedict offers obvious advice: *remember that you die.* Who can forget that life, like pouring cream, comes with an expiration date? Who ignores that bodies can't be refrigerated forever? I think of death on the spring day Camille leaves me to cross a busy street corner and walk two blocks to a friend's house. The robins are out, pulling fat worms from ground sodden from last night's rain. My daughter is seventeen, long-legged, capable. In three weeks, she will take her final high school exams. In three months, she will be spun out into a world of independence. Still, I can't help but issue stern warnings about "crossing at the crosswalk" and "looking both ways." I am a mother, and the hanging sword of Damocles is my business.

Remember that you die.

Denial of death was humanity's first seduction. "You will not surely die," the serpent flattered Eve in Genesis 3:4, plying her with lies of endless, ageless life, time unfurling like infinite spools of golden thread. It's this lie, this forked tongue I think of when I sit in the waiting room of a local dermatology office, thumbing through advertisements for chemical peels and microdermabrasion and Botox. It's this lie, this forked tongue I think of when I'm seated on the examining table, my face scrutinized under glaring magnification. *Mmm,* the doctor murmurs, her thumb and forefinger pinching skin. I am forty-six and interested mostly in fading the hyperpigmented spots on my cheeks and upper lip, but I am tempted—*tempted*—to pay good money for so much more.

Remember that you die.

We could wonder about the urgency of Benedict's pessimism. Why rain on life's parade prematurely? But it's wisdom that demands realism. If time will be lived well and wisely, days must be numbered, measured realistically as a mere handsbreadth. Wisdom alone can lift and wield the heavy blade of *decision*, this word whose Latin root means "cut off" or "kill." Choosing is murder—because time will not afford every opportunity.

I could better appreciate this grief, this violence, when, for months, I kept a "Yes/No/Wish I could" list. I quickly discovered that no time management system could possibly create the needed margin for all those wishes. To be human is to leave good undone, and there is no cure for the gnawing regret I share with the speaker in Robert Frost's famous poem, "The Road Not Taken." Though normally we read this poem as an argument for heroically taking untraveled paths, what's clearer is the poem's portrayal of the human predicament, entangled as we are in the briars of time: "Two roads diverged in a yellow wood / And sorry I could not travel both."[3]

As the purple haze of evening fades into black, the books are finally reshelved, and Heather and I are resettled into armchairs. We talk about some of those roads we thought to keep for another day. Heather worked hard to put her husband through seminary, a second master's degree, then a PhD program without loans. This had been "their" decision. It wasn't until they'd had their first child that she realized "their" decision had foreclosed on her own academic dreams. "I was resentful once," she admits to me. "But then I think to myself: I chose something else."

Frost's poem again: "I doubted if I should ever come back."[4]

Both of us nearing fifty, Heather and I know to admit that earthly life is not open-ended possibility. Our advice, then, is rather practical: for as many days as you're given, delight in them. Wear your yeses to a nub. Let your brimming cup of joy, even in the long, dark valleys of *no* and *wish I could*, bear witness to the God who enjoys you.

But then remember: like a cord, time will be cut. The lights will go out. The curtains will draw. This stage on which life is played will be swept by the night custodian, and the only one to remember your name will be God himself. The God who remembers Abraham, Noah, Rahab.[5] The God who remembers every sworn promise of love. Remember that you die—and grow lionhearted.

Life is a mist, a vapor, a disappearing storm cloud—*hebel*, in the biblical Hebrew. Remember life is as vain as beauty is fleeting. Not meaningless but short. This habit of remembering death can save your life. It can spare you the harrow of the scene described in the book of Daniel: King Belshazzar and his court eating, drinking, and generally being merry. With the looted goblets of Solomon's temple, they imbibe the wine of tomfoolery. *Death will not come. Not now. Not for us.*

When a ghostly hand scrawls judgment on the wall, aging Daniel is hurried to the feast by the queen. His reputation for wisdom precedes him. "You will die," he tells the king. Belshazzar has been weighed in the balances and found wanting. His kingdom will be divided and given to the Medes and the Persians. "You have praised the gods of silver and gold, of bronze, iron, wood, and stone, which do not see or hear or know, but the God in whose hand is your breath, and whose are all your ways, you have not honored."[6]

In all the days he was given, tragically the great king did not bow to the Giver of time.

Fitting Time

In Oliver Burkeman's recent book *Four Thousand Weeks: Time Management for Mortals,* he does not paint with the apocalyptic strokes of Daniel, even if his introduction is morbidly titled "In the Long Run, We're All Dead." Neither does Burkeman offer any certainty about the monumental tasks of living and dying—certainly no urgency about the one to whom all time is owed. In fact, Burkeman can only gesture vaguely at the meaning he says we yearn for, the "important and fulfilling ways we could be spending our time."[7]

Like many time management books, Burkeman's book does not answer the biggest, most pressing questions of time: the ones about choosing the good. He does, however, acknowledge the impasse of time management advice. Time management can optimize our productivity and performance, but it cannot relieve our existential anguish. We will die. And for those of us without the money to endow chairs or fund hospital wings, our names will die with us.

Time isn't something to be managed—not with death in view. Yes, we can get more organized with our projects. Yes, we can be more deliberate about our calendar commitments. Yes, we can spend our attention more mindfully, rather than scrolling social media and binge-watching reality TV. But for all these temporary goods, time management cannot and will not prevent our incurable condition.

In the face of death, we don't need more productive time. We need to discover the practice of *fitting time*.

I learn about fitting time from Craig Bartholomew's commentary on Ecclesiastes—or at least I learn what I can't learn even after the exegetes have worked the text like dough. It takes multiple readings of the chapter discussing Ecclesiastes 3 and "The Mystery of Time" before I understand that I'm probably not meant to understand the complexities scholars are still debating. I'm not even talking about the obviously hard parts. I'm talking about a verse as seemingly straightforward as the second half of verse 11: "Also, he has put eternity into man's heart, yet so that he cannot find out what God has done from the beginning to the end."

For one, scholars can't decide on the meaning of "eternity." Contenders are: the world, a sense of past and future, a sense of duration, ignorance, distant time, and consciousness of the eternal.[8] The only agreement, in the whole of the chapter, seems to be that the "time" and "season" and "eternity" cited here are "God's times, not our times."[9]

"Wisdom," Bartholomew writes, "involves knowing the fitting time."[10] In part, fitting time requires us to make sense of life's seasonality, poetically framed for us in Ecclesiastes 3. Fitting time bears no illusions about death. "For everything there is a season," the Teacher writes. A time to plant and to pluck up. A time to break down and to build. A time to weep and to laugh.

A time to be born—and a time to die.[11]

As a writer, I can't help but think how *fitting* it is that this text comes to us in the form of a sonnet. Sonnets, like time, demand the exercise of creativity within constraint. Fitting time recognizes the moral bounds of a universe created by God. We are free to decide—but not free to do as we please. Wisdom in the Bible always assumes human beings in right relationship with God, with neighbor, with self. It assumes "appropriate time" and "appointed time," even "good time."

Poetry is not, of course, a primarily rational enterprise. Its goal isn't argument but effect. Its methods aren't logic but rhyme and meter and sound. Poetry distills life as image—and maybe that's where time always leaves us. With trees, for example, which cause us to remember Psalm 1, this overture of wisdom in our ancient book of prayers.

Living good time, living fitting time, is the lifelong enterprise of the oak, the pine, the cedar, the redwood. In the wisdom text of Psalm 1, we're instructed to patiently send our roots down deep into the good, wise words of the Lord. These words presumably teach us how to live time well. They inspire us to grow leaves and fruit and *feed someone*.

And if the Beguines were right, these medieval women who prayed and fasted and bustled about rescuing the prostitutes, clothing the beggars, raising the orphans, feeding the poor, caring for the sick, keeping vigil at the bed of the dying, then Christ is this ancient oak. He is the blessed man of Psalm 1.

Because all time tells a story, the center of this story is Jesus of Nazareth: dead and buried, risen and returning. Unlike the Teacher in Ecclesiastes, who left us with a fair degree of cynicism about the profit of earthly life and labor, "we have the full revelation in Christ, and this provides the grand story within which it is possible to live and to discern what is fitting and wise."[12] Christ, the wisdom of God—in you, in me, the hope of glory.

Productivity doesn't qualify any difference between the minutes, the hours, the days, the years. It equalizes time. It measures the minutes uniformly. Fitting time, on the other hand, proposes a very different framework. It doesn't measure the "reward" and "waste" of time by what it produces. Fitting time recognizes the relative value of an hour or a year. It acknowledges that time spent productively—and inopportunely—is time misspent. It recognizes time spent efficiently—and ignorant of time's larger story—is wasted time.

The task of discerning fitting time demands wisdom. What does this moment require of us? What opportunities, should we neglect them, might prove irretrievable? Mortal time is a spool, and it will not, for all our efforts, be rewound.

On the one hand, it may sometimes be fitting for me to hole myself up in my basement office, with my "Please Do Not Disturb" sign on my closed door. And on the other hand, sometimes interruptions won't be put off. Sometimes they hail like heaven-sent stones. Sometimes these interruptions are your aging mother. Sometimes they are your dying friend.

What's fitting for my week at Heather's house, I know, is the hours nearing midnight we spend talking. What's fitting is the butternut squash soup I make for Sunday lunch, Heather, her son, Andrew, and I eating in the dining room whose windows afford a glimpse of the sea. What is fitting is Tuesday morning, when I carry various pieces of furniture from room to room and my friend and I consider measurements for new rugs. What is fitting is that I am here after I have worried about not seeing Heather again. What is fitting is trusting God for the work I've left behind.

This time is a gift, and it is given for now.

Fear Not

I am dying too. At least I think I must be dying when my doctor calls on a Friday afternoon, hours after I've had a follow-up mammogram and ultrasound. I think of this lump we have been monitoring for more than a year, this loaf we have been watching to see rise. "Next steps are that we'll send you to the cancer clinic at the hospital," my doctor says. "They'll likely repeat the images before the biopsy."

Less than a week later, I take the elevator to the fourth floor of Sunnybrook Hospital. I know to memorize the details of the curtained stall where I change into my paper gown. I know to recall the sweaty odor of the windowless room where a tight-lipped Eastern European woman performs the procedure. I know to obey the sign posted on the wall that informs me I must not ask the technician any questions.

I record all these details—because I know I am going to die.

I think of my death as I hold my arms above my head, like a hostage. The technician squeezes cold jelly onto my right breast. The machine whirs. I shiver, understanding how this part of my body that once fed life into my children can be made to tell ineluctable time, the time we don't ever escape. For forty-five minutes, the technician wands her way clockwise. One o'clock. Two o'clock. Three o'clock—and somewhere, between family dinner and another episode of *The Great British Baking Show,* she scowls. Adds more jelly. Retraces the clock face. Searches the seconds.

Remember that you die.

But I'm not dying, I learn after that appointment. At least not from breast cancer and not right now. I have been catastrophizing again. After the death of my father and the suicide of my brother, I can't seem to help this habit. Death has always been with me in their absence. In my life, death is air, is gravity, is the wavelength of sound and light.

I know how easily you can accommodate yourself to the fright that the universe is just this threadbare, that you and those you love might fall through any minute. But I also know the paradox that it is not a fright at all. You gain sanity for not hoping in permanence. You grow wise for remembering you will die.

Hope is possible, even here at the bottom—because as a Christian, you understand death is not the end.

I think of the medieval statue of Jesus awaiting the resurrection that is housed in the Princely Collections at the Liechtenstein Garden Palace in Vienna. The helpful museum staff tells me this statue is called "Christ of the Holy Sepulchre."[13] I visited the small private collection while in Vienna with my husband and the top sales performers in his company, the ones I was always bothering for productivity advice. "How do you spend your time?" I asked during those dinners when my husband was pulled away by the elbow. I always imagined these hard-driving men and women had some secret incantation for materializing time out of thin air.

The statue's wood is weathered, the paint faded except for the faint red of Jesus's lips and wounds. He looks as if he is dreaming sweetly behind his closed eyes. What I found so striking about the statue—and why I pestered the curator for more information about it after we'd returned home—was that it was not the sagging figure of Good Friday Jesus, hanging from the cross, nor was it the triumphal figure of Easter morning Jesus, raised from the dead. It was the Christ of Holy Saturday, the Christ of the time being.

> The dead body of Christ is laid out as though he was sleeping. His nimbus disc also serves as a pillow, and the corpse is wrapped in a delicate cloth which—except for the chest area with the side wound, the forearms and the bearded face— covers the figure with delicate flowing folds. His hands pierced by the nails of the cross are laid on his thighs with convulsively spread fingers, but the gentle swaying of the body as a whole reduces the impression of rigor mortis.[14]

Unlike the other Christs of medieval devotional art, this Christ is a waiting Christ.

Reading later about other similar works of the fourteenth century, I learn this life-size statue likely played a role in Paschal celebrations. The priest would have placed a small piece of the host in the open wound of Jesus's side on Maundy Thursday. Then this small crust of bread would have been retrieved on Easter morning before the church, at the very moment the angelic announcement at the empty tomb was dramatized before the congregants: "He is not here. He is risen today!"

Remember that you die, the Easter play warns. Then—*comfort, comfort my people*—remember that you live.[15]

Last night, reading the foreword to a book of prayers on death, grief, and hope given to me by a friend who recently lost her mother, I remember this hope. "In the face of our own deaths, or the deaths of those we are privileged to know most in this pilgrimage, we all need to be reminded again and again of this great story and its storied end."[16]

Christ's body was broken, was buried—and then was resurrected and retrieved. And the good news, *the gospel*, of this story is that death is no longer a terror or mortal dread. No, we don't hope to get cancer or COVID—but we don't cower in their shadow. If we have believing trust in the resurrected, retrieved, and returning Christ, we are saved not just from death but from our fear of death. Christ has harrowed the gates of hell itself, as the Apostles' Creed reminds us, and whatever that exactly means (because I'm not at all sure), I think it means we fear not.

Fear not.

Firmness of Purpose

When journalist, civil rights activist, and suffragist Ida B. Wells wrote in her journal on her twenty-fifth birthday, she had already acquired a sense of time's passing and the purposefulness she would need for the time that remained: "As this day's arrival enables me to count the twenty fifth milestone, I go back over them in memory and review my life." A whole quarter century: Wells took inventory. She remembered.

> There is nothing for which I lament the wasted opportunities as I do my neglect to pick up the crumbs of knowledge that were within my reach. Consequently I find myself at this age as deficient in a comprehensive knowledge as the veriest school-girl just entering the higher course. I heartily deplore the neglect. God grant I may be given firmness of purpose sufficient to essay and continue its eradication! Thou knowest I hunger & thirst after righteousness & knowledge. O, give me the steadiness of purpose, the will to acquire both. Twenty-five years old today! May another 10 years find me increased in honesty & purity of purpose & motive![17]

Ida B. Wells figures among the ten African American women featured in Jasmine Holmes's wonderful book *Carved in Ebony*. Wells was born a slave in Mississippi in 1862, and the privileges of time management were not her inheritance. It's clear, however, that at age twenty-five Wells was committed to harnessing the power of intention. She knew obedience to God required it.

Heather and I were Wells's age when we met at Arlington Heights Evangelical Free Church. We were not standing in front of the mirror, as today, and seeing gray roots. We were sailing into the adventure called adulting.

Twenty years later, when I visit Heather in Scotland, we have teenagers and aging parents, regrets and still-stubborn plans. During my visit, Heather wants my help to think about changes to this house that had once been the village doctor's family residence, the house referred to as being "above the old surgery." Should they open the wall to the kitchen pantry for more light? Should they reconfigure the stove, the sink? Should they tear down the wall behind the stairs, which had served to close off some of the first-floor rooms for family quarters when the house had operated as a bed and breakfast? We don't get around to paint colors and to putting up the Christmas tree. Because time goes too fast.

In the longest longitudinal study of human flourishing, begun at Harvard in 1938, it's been concluded that human relationships are a critically important factor in human health and well-being. I think we intuitively know this. And yet it's noteworthy how little regard is given to human relationships in a lot of time management advice.

I look back at my Kindle copy of *Getting Things Done* and search "friendship." It turns up no results. I find references to "community" only a couple of times, and those are listed under "projects." I search "love" and find two references to "loved ones" and "those you love." But mostly, love is directed elsewhere. There are the "organizing tools you love to use." There are the "fun and creative things you'd love to start exploring."

"You actually love to do a thing as long as you get the feeling you've completed something."[18]

Friendship and love, like spiritual formation, aren't projects to complete. Maybe they always feel unfinished, too aspirational for the finitude of our lives.

In the spring, when I think I am dying, I go looking for writing by Puritan women and find a letter from a mother who died after delivering twins. *The Copy of a Valedictory and Monitory Writing* was written in the seventeenth century by Sarah Goodhue and "found after her decease; full of spiritual experiences, sage counsels, pious instructions, and serious exhortations."[19]

Sarah's first concern in the letter is for her husband, Joseph, who "hast a great family of children, and some of them small." Sarah's not sure he'll manage, deprived of her help, so she instructs him to give this new child (or children, as they turned out to be) to her parents, then give away another two of the remaining eight to other family members: John to cousin Symond Stacy and Susanna to cousin Catharine Whipple. After these bequests, Sarah turns to address first her parents, with gratitude, then her fellow Christians, and finally her children, "which in pains and care have cost [her] dear." She admonishes them to fear God, to love Christ best, to read the Bible, and to marry only those who "as first do seek the kingdom of heaven." She implores her children to pray for God to improve their privileges, namely those of youth.

> For you know not how soon your health may be turned into sickness, your strength into weakness, and your lives into death; as death cuts the tree of your life down, so it will lie; as death leaveth you, so judgment will find you out.[20]

Remember that you die, Sarah tells her children.

I start my own letter to my oldest daughter from the hospital. "Sitting here, my hospital gown open to the front, the ties loosening and needing to be reknotted," I write, "I am growing cold. I consider how to make time for regular chemotherapy appointments. I picture myself bald. I pledge to let my hair grow back gray. I promise to wear, as often as the mood strikes, my brightest shade of lipstick and my baggiest pair of sweatpants."

I swear, for once, forever, to let go of every falsehood and flattery. It may yet be mine to decide when to stop coloring my hair and, as they say, *let myself go.*

Backward Glance

"There's a tree I want to show you at St. Mary's College," Heather tells me a couple of days before I leave. St. Mary's is home to St. Andrews faculty and school of divinity, where her husband, Dave, works.

St. Andrews is the oldest university in Scotland, and St. Mary's College was founded in the sixteenth century. Although a fire damaged many of the buildings in 1727, the stone of their replacements still signals the solidity of centuries. When I follow Heather slowly up the spiraling stone stairs to the second floor of one of the buildings, I worry for her. The treads of some of the stairs are dangerously narrow, and she is trying to manage with her crutch. "No, no, I'm fine," she says as she waves with her free hand, refusing any help.

The great holm oak at the center of St. Mary's quadrangle was planted in the mid-eighteenth century. It is not nearly as old as the smaller thorn tree—or hawthorn bush—growing at the foot of the Founder's Tower. Mary Queen of Scots is said to have planted this tree in the 1560s. It leans slightly, borne up by crutches, but still bears fruit in the fall.

This November day is blustery, and the winds portend winter. Nevertheless, the leaves of the holm oak are still clinging to its branches, still coloring the enormous canopy green. Poking around on the internet later, I learn that this species of oak is an evergreen, its leaves "waxy like those of a rhododendron." I stand there, taking pictures, and think of the women and men bent over books in the classrooms of these stone buildings, studying the great theological minds of the ages. Maybe even now they are opening Augustine and meditating, as he did more than fifteen hundred years ago, on the nature of time.

When I first read Augustine's *Confessions* years ago, I skipped all the protracted passages about time. Lately, though, I've been returning to them. "I confess to you, Lord, that I still do not know what time is, and I further confess to you, Lord, that as I say this I know myself to be conditioned by time."[21] Augustine acknowledges that time induces suffering. We are made subject "to change and variation."[22] He knows that the weight of time bows and bends the trees, that it bows and bends our decaying bodies.

Yet God is eternal—and this is our hope, even in time's grief. "Then shall I find stability and solidity in you," Augustine writes.[23] God, the beginning. God, the end. God, the beginning again.

Let the person who understands this make confession to you. How exalted you are, and the humble in heart are your house. You lift up those who are cast down and those whom you raise to that summit which is yourself do not fall.[24]

I can't help but think of Moses and Psalm 90, the mountains far younger than God.

Maybe all the mystics have tried pondering time, wondering exactly how God's eternal purposes are related to our temporal lives. Julian of Norwich tried to understand the relationship of past and present and future, seeing in her first revelation that a small hazelnut held in the palm of her hand represented God's care for "all that is made." Nothing is despised for its "littleness," she concludes. Julian held that small seed in her hand and remembered the scope of God's good time. "It lasteth and ever shall, for God loveth it. And so hath all thing being by the love of God."[25] If God never worries after tomorrow, never wrings his hands over yesterday, there's surely no cause for fear.

Heather and I are back in the car. The winds are growing fiercer, and the sky is growing darker. It's even starting to snow. We will pick up more sweet potatoes on our drive back to Anstruther, so that I can make the casserole she'll take for an American Thanksgiving celebration after I'm gone. Tomorrow I will wing my way back to Toronto, like a tiny helicopter seed.

Behind us, the great holm oak grows smaller. The wind wrests acorns from its branches. It makes me remember that wood carving of Christ on Holy Saturday. Here he is, the Blessed Man of Psalm 1, awaiting the resurrection. "There shall come forth a shoot from the stump of Jesse, and a branch from his roots shall bear fruit."[26] The promise of God was buried a seed and raised a tree.

I could count God's time slow. Or I could try keeping it.

TO CONSIDER

Is death something difficult or easy for you to remember? What scares you about this habit of remembering death?

What story does the death, resurrection, and return of Jesus Christ tell about time? And what trouble, if any, do you have believing that story?

How would the habit of remembering death change your everyday habits and life ambitions, if at all?

TO PRAY

Father, you are the everlasting God—Maker of the mountains and Creator of time. We often avoid thinking of life's brevity because there is much on earth we love and hate to lose. Help us to practice time's mystery, fully entering today with holy intention, all the while remembering that tomorrow is only yours to give. Thank you for Jesus Christ, standing at the center of time's story, who makes it possible to hope in life beyond the grave.

AFTERWORD

In Which I Don't Give Up Reading
Time Management Books

I don't know what time it is, by which I mean I'm ignorant of the Christian calendar. For the entire season following Epiphany, we argue about it at the dining room table.

"Epiphany, Day 34," my husband reads from our prayer book. Andrew looks knowingly at me, then loudly corrects his father. "Ordinary Time, Day 33." The long-standing family dispute, or at least one lasting more than four weeks, is whether Epiphany is a single day, which I've understood after researching for this book, or a longer season, which is the stance taken by *Seeking God's Face*, a copy of which Ryan holds in his hand.

Neither Ryan nor I were raised in church traditions that observed the feasts and fasts of the Christian calendar. I was a cradle Southern Baptist. Growing up, I thought Advent and Lent belonged to the Episcopalians, which gave me reason enough to suspect it. I may be Presbyterian now, but this doesn't mean I know much more than when I was a child, when all of time was ordinary and the calendar was organized around Sunday school and choir practice, Hallmark holidays and patriotic observances, fall revival and summer camp.

It wasn't until I began reading my new copy of *The Oxford Companion to the Year* that I started seeing there is nothing ordinary about time at all, no matter your religious persuasion. This heavy volume explores "calendar customs" and "time reckoning," mostly from a Western—and particularly British—perspective. I learned all kinds of arcane information about my birthday, May 12. It's the official foundation date of Constantinople, in AD 330. Pancratius, a Roman Catholic saint, was allegedly martyred under Diocletian on this date at age fourteen, and he can be "invoked against cramps." May 12 is also the purported date of a witch festival where witches ride their broomsticks in the air and wreak general havoc in fields and homes.[1]

And here I thought May 12 was simply the day I was delivered into the arms of my mother, the best gift she ever received on Mother's Day.

The obvious chagrin I find in this heavy volume is that our calendar has an invincibly Christian history. "It will not please all readers to be reminded," the editors write,

> that the calendar of ancient Rome has become the modern international standard as a result of Christianity; those to whom these facts are offensive may care to devise, and then persuade the human race to use, a truly non-sectarian and politically neutral calendar.[2]

It's a bit of a cheeky dare on their part, considering just such a project miserably failed when attempted by the former Soviet Union.

In 1929, under Lenin's decree, the Christian calendar was abolished and with it the seven-day week. The year was divided into twelve months of thirty days, each divided into six weeks of five working days. The communist regime wasn't going to give workers a weekend—of leisure, of worship—even if they could have one in five days off: "Propaganda posters showed the bourgeois idlers Saturday and Sunday being pitched out of doors."[3] Lenin's antireligious calendar was amended after two years. It was abandoned in another nine.[4]

Timekeeping has never been a neutral exercise. Not today, when everyone is working for the weekend. Not a hundred years ago, when Sabbath laws were still in force. The history of timekeeping is a history of technology, of empire building, of capitalism, of power, of morality, of waxing and waning faith. "A history of clocks is a history of civilization," argues David Rooney in *About Time.*[5]

To have arrived where we are today, when "productivity" and "efficiency" have displaced *sola deo gloria,* is to chart a movement not unlike the one astronomers have charted throughout human history. They've tried telling time by reading the sky.

To tell time is to tell a certain kind of story. Where does time begin? Where might time lead? Are we hopelessly adrift in time, without a sense of origin or destiny? Are we fated to repeat cycles of recurrence, hoping to—eventually—get it right? In my own life, especially when I've been trapped in a productivity mindset, I've seen that time is anxiety and misfortune, indecision and regret.

As a Christian, however, I've also discovered time is hope.

When Paul crisscrossed the ancient Roman Empire, traveling on his missionary journeys, he brought time's good news. Jesus is God! These first-century pagans, influenced by the Epicureanism and Stoicism of their day, needed to unlearn certain habits of timekeeping. They needed to learn that God had acted in history to rescue and redeem a people for himself, that once death was finally put under the feet of Jesus, the world would finally begin again under his rule. The real "golden age" would not be ushered in by another Caesar. It had begun with the appearing of the Messiah—his death and resurrection.

Unlike these early pagan converts to Christianity, first-century Jewish converts knew that time was teleological, that it was headed somewhere purposeful. But like the pagans, they also had unlearning and relearning to do. Israel had long been a waiting people. After their exile from the land, they were waiting on God to make good on his promises to return them home. With the arrival of John the Baptist, an end to waiting was announced, a beginning heralded. The kingdom was at hand![6]

First-century Christians understood faith called them to tell time differently. It's something many of us have yet to learn.

I wish I'd considered the story I was telling about time far earlier than now, at midlife, although maybe there's an inevitability to that delinquency. It takes time for wisdom to grow. I fear I've been far too preoccupied with getting things done. I've hurried past people and procrastinated on important matters of discipleship. I wish someone had given me (and my husband) a good shake the first year of our marriage and taught us to live time fittingly. We might have continued with our graduate degrees—and also have made time for more regular date nights. I wish someone had, in my dark seasons of grief, told me to slow down, to be gentle with myself, to be patient with grief, which isn't a thing to be rushed. When my children were young and running madly through the aisles of Trader Joe's, searching for the purple monkey, I wish I had believed all the dear old ladies that *the days were long and the years were short.*

It's this last regret I write about in a poem to my daughter Audrey on her sixteenth birthday:

> I wish I'd caught those days by their tail,
> Pinned them down for one good look.
> I should have squeezed tight
> The sight of wispy hair and stubby legs,
> Of you not-yet-big and grown out of my arms.

This, for me, might be time's greatest pain. I don't ultimately worry about failing to get things done. I'm too type A for that. I worry that time is irretrievable. I lie awake with regret, moving through memories like old slides. I am haunted by the time I've lived and can no longer affect.

Regret is the thing that stabbed recently when I read the story of Joseph in Genesis. Usually, when my Bible reading plan returns me to this story in the month of January, I put myself in the shoes of the younger, persecuted brother.

This year, however, I was caught up in the tornado of the older brothers' emotions.

When they are treated roughly by Joseph upon arriving in Egypt, looking for food and accused of being spies, they know why: "We are guilty concerning our brother, in that we saw the distress of his soul, when he begged us and we did not listen."[7] Hebrew scholar Robert Alter renders this verse even more poetically: "Alas, we are guilty for our brother, whose mortal distress we saw when he pleaded with us and we did not listen."[8]

I could see that the brothers weren't simply recalling the day's events from all those years ago. No, they were reliving the memory of wanting Joseph dead. They were seeing to the bottom of that hole into which they'd thrown him like an animal. They were hearing his hoarse and plaintive pleas as they held his wondrous coat in their hands.

I haven't committed these brothers' treachery, but I am guilty nonetheless. I could stack them up, all these *wish I hads*.

I know what St. Benedict would tell me to do when I am pinned down by those *if-onlys* and *what-ifs*. I read it in his rule: "As soon as wrongful thoughts come into your heart, dash them against Christ."[9] Benedict reminds me that I cannot rewind time by my efforts—but time will be made new through Christ's.

Ultimately, I think regret, when it spirals into shame and self-condemnation, is a defeating proposition. We are not, after all, imprisoned in time, fated to keep practicing our familiar patterns of vice. Time is made new, and we are made new in it. And we don't simply breathe a sigh of relief that offense has been erased, our sin cast into the bottom of the ocean. We pledge ourselves to the lifelong process of conversion. Because we are saved by mercy and for mercy's sake.

That process—plodding, fitful, slow—bears the ripened fruit of wisdom.

It was my friend Heather who introduced me to Ellen Davis's book *Getting Involved with God*. In her chapter on the book of Proverbs, Davis writes about how Proverbs was almost left out of the Hebrew Bible. First-century rabbis couldn't see the spiritual importance of the commonsense wisdom of this book. I, of course, can't help remembering Proverbs was the book that rained stones on my head as it crowed about my responsibilities to care for my aging mother.

Do not despise your mother when she is old!

(I got it, Lord.)

Unlike their Egyptian and Mesopotamian counterparts, who studied astronomy, architecture, engineering, medicine, and the fine arts, ancient Israel was far more concerned with practical affairs. Davis explains:

> [Proverbs] is a book for unexceptional people trying to live wisely and faithfully in the generally undramatic circumstances of daily life, on the days when water does not pour forth out of rocks and angels do not come to lunch. The Israelite sages are concerned with the same things we worry about, the things people regularly consult their pastors and friends about: how to avoid bitter domestic quarrels, what to tell your friends about sex and about God, what to do when somebody asks you to lend them money,

how to handle your own money and your work life, how to cultivate lasting friendships.[10]

Wisdom Literature is preoccupied with matters of time. I can see today why my interest in Wisdom Literature has grown. It has everything to do with the task called life. It's a response to God's self-revelation, and it is required for ordinary time. The good news is that wisdom is God's enthusiastic gift to his people. We ask—and he grants. This isn't to say he gives it in the form of Julia Child's *Mastering the Art of French Cooking*. No, life is not a recipe. Most often, it's the risky proposition of deciding. We take up salt, fish, knife—and hear God shush our fears about getting things exactly right. *Patience*, he says.

It will take practice.

I had to Google to learn that the church's color for Ordinary Time is green, that *ordinary* does not mean "routine" or "unextraordinary" but instead refers to the ordinal numbers used to name and count the Sundays after the Christmas and Easter cycles. *Tempus ordinarium* is Latin for "numbered time." But despite all the learning I did for writing this book, I never settled the argument at the dinner table about whether Epiphany is a day or litany of days.

Maybe it doesn't really matter.

I wonder, finishing these pages, if I'll give up on reading time management books, which enforce a strict rule for numbering time in productive units. *Probably not*, I admit. I'll read them, haplessly interested in taming the unruliness of my busy life. I know that, like the fern I watched my mom replant and reposition, life has a habit for outgrowing pots and demanding my creative love. But I won't thumb the pages of those books, looking for time.

Because now I know where time is kept. And now I know for sure who's keeping it.

ACKNOWLEDGMENTS

Books aren't only written; like the hours, they're inherited and received. I only wish I could remember all the hands through which this book has passed.

First, Lauren Winner and other writers read embryonic writing for this book during a Glen workshop. I am grateful for their instructive feedback, especially about sources and writing with care about bodies. Thank you.

Susanne Paula Antonetta read many chapters as my mentor in the MFA program at Seattle Pacific University. When I wanted to give up on this book entirely, she gently encouraged me to keep going. Thank you. And I am thankful, too, for the community of writers at SPU of which I'm so grateful to be a part.

There are so many writing friends and colleagues who sent recommendations for books and podcasts and articles: Ashley Hales, Amber Bowen, Bill DeJong, Darryl Dash, Charity Singleton Craig, Ted Olsen, Amy Julia Becker, Chris Smith, Joel Wentz, Bronwyn Lea, Laura Fabrycky. I couldn't possibly name all the readers of Post Script, too, who sent ideas and encouragement. Thank you.

Heather Moffitt has been a constant conversation partner, especially now that I've persuaded her, since my trip to Scotland, to trade messages on Voxer. Her friendship is a joy—her witness of faith a gift. Thank you.

I hope it's evident from my endnotes that I've benefited enormously from the good work of scholars. For those like me who have not had the time to consecrate ourselves to the kind of deep work you engage, thank you.

Thank you, Baker Books, for your partnership in taking this book from seed to fruiting tree. Stephanie Smith, thanks for continually pushing me to consider narrative arc and for helping me overcome my persistent self-doubt. Laura Palma, thanks for catching an early vision for cover design—and thanks to Eleanore Lubbers, for your illustration. Lindsey Spoolstra, thanks for helping me achieve clarity and ensure accurate citation. To my many other unsung publishing heroes, including the enthusiastic marketing team: thank you.

My spiritual director, Beth Booram, is a living example of time-full living and listening. Thank you.

My agent, Lisa Jackson, did not despair when I promised a proposal I never delivered. Thank you.

My small group—Ken and Seong, Gwen and Paul, Dave and Shen, Mabel and Jerry, Anne-Pascale and Emanuel—prayed for this work and encouraged me in it. Thank you.

My daughter Audrey read early drafts and helped me see places where the writing fell flat. Thank you. My other children suffered many dinner conversations about time (and acedia). I couldn't be prouder that you know the meaning of this old word. Thank you.

My husband, Ryan, sat hours, listening to me read aloud when I finally had my first finished draft. Thank you.

Most of all, I thank God for his help and the ordinary miracle these pages represent. On paper, there was not enough time to write this book. Then again, paper, like a clock, tells only a partial truth.

Thank you.

NOTES

In the Year of Our Lord 2020

1. Psalm 90:10.
2. Isaiah 40:21, 22, 24.
3. Laurie Penny, "Productivity Is Not Working," *Wired*, April 17, 2020, https://www.wired.com/story/question-productivity-coronavirus/.
4. Anne Ortlund, *Disciplines of the Beautiful Woman* (Nashville: W Publishing, 1984), 65.
5. Stephen Marche, "The Hollow Patriarchy," in *The Unmade Bed* (New York: Simon & Schuster, 2017), Kindle ed.
6. Jeremy Taylor, "Chapter 1," in *The Rule and Exercises of Holy Living*, https://quod.lib.umich.edu/e/eebo/A64109.0001.001/1:6.1.1?rgn=div3;view=fulltext.
7. Matthew 6:27.
8. I have in my mind here the subtitle of Ashley Hales's good book, *A Spacious Life: Trading Hustle and Hurry for the Goodness of Limits* (Downers Grove, IL: InterVarsity, 2021).
9. Jen A. Miller, "Why You Should Start a Coronavirus Diary," *New York Times*, updated October 7, 2021, https://www.nytimes.com/2020/04/13/smarter-living/why-you-should-start-a-coronavirus-diary.html.

YOLO

1. Psalm 130:5–6.
2. Ephesians 2:1 NIV.
3. L. S. Dugdale, *The Lost Art of Dying* (New York: HarperOne, 2020), 11.
4. Ephesians 2:4–5 NIV.
5. Hebrews 3:15.
6. Ephesians 2:10 NIV.

7. Ephesians 2:6 NIV.

8. I heard this phrase—from Hildegard of Bingen—in a message given by Amy Peterson at the fall 2020 MFA residency for Seattle Pacific University.

9. Melissa Gregg, *Counterproductive* (Durham, NC: Duke University Press, 2018), x.

10. Laura Vanderkam, *I Know How She Does It: How Successful Women Make the Most of Their Time* (New York: Portfolio, 2017).

11. Matt Perman, *What's Best Next* (Grand Rapids: Zondervan, 2014), 19.

12. Jen Pollock Michel, "Maybe Jesus Wants Us to Get Things Done," *Christianity Today*, May 2, 2014, https://www.christianitytoday.com/ct/2014/may-web-only/maybe-jesus-wants-us-to-get-things-done.html.

13. Gregg, *Counterproductive*, 55.

14. As quoted in Gregg, *Counterproductive*, 26.

15. Gregg, *Counterproductive*, 33.

16. Clive Thompson, "Hundreds of Ways to Get S#!+ Done—and We Still Don't," *Wired*, July 27, 2021, https://www.wired.com/story/to-do-apps-failed-productivity-tools/.

17. Thompson, "Hundreds of Ways to Get S#!+ Done."

18. Thompson, "Hundreds of Ways to Get S#!+ Done."

Life Hack

1. Proverbs 1:7.

2. Ellen Davis, *Getting Involved with God: Rediscovering the Old Testament* (Cambridge, MA: Cowley, 2001), 91.

3. Psalm 32:9.

4. Derek Kidner, "God and Man," in *Proverbs*, Kidner Classic Commentaries series (Downers Grove, IL: IVP Academic, 2008), Kindle ed.

5. Kidner, "God and Man."

6. Derek Kidner, "The Book of Proverbs: A Life Well Managed," in *The Wisdom of Proverbs, Job, and Ecclesiastes* (Downers Grove, IL: IVP Academic, 1985), Kindle ed.

7. Derek Kidner, "Meeting of Minds," in *The Wisdom of Proverbs, Job, and Ecclesiastes.*

8. Kidner, "Meeting of Minds."

9. Ellen Davis, "Introduction to Proverbs," in *Proverbs, Ecclesiastes, and the Song of Songs* (Louisville: Westminster John Knox, 2000), Kindle ed.

10. Oliver Burkeman, *Four Thousand Weeks: Time Management for Mortals* (New York: Farrar, Straus & Giroux, 2021).

11. Gregg, *Counterproductive*, 9.

12. Gregg, *Counterproductive*, 32.

13. Sara Hendren, *What Can a Body Do?: How We Meet the Built World* (New York: Riverhead, 2020), 166.

14. Ellen Samuels, "Six Ways of Looking at Crip Time," *Disability Studies Quarterly* 37, no. 3 (2017), https://dsq-sds.org/article/view/5824/4684.

15. I've benefited enormously to learn from John Swinton, *Becoming Friends of Time: Disability, Timefullness, and Gentle Discipleship* (Waco: Baylor University, 2016).

16. Hendren, *What Can a Body Do?*, 182.

On Living the Lord's Time

1. Alexandros Papadiamandis, "A Pilgrimage to Kastro," in *The Boundless Garden* (Limni, Evia, Greece: Denise Harvey, 2007), 106.

2. Papadiamandis, "Pilgrimage to Kastro," 104.

3. N. T. Wright, *Paul* (San Francisco: HarperOne, 2018), 18.

4. Exodus 20:2.

5. David Zahl, "Introduction," in *Seculosity* (Minneapolis: Fortress, 2019), Kindle ed.

6. Psalm 115:8.

7. Psalm 121:2, 8.

8. See my book *Keeping Place* (Downers Grove, IL: InterVarsity, 2016).

9. Acts 17:26.

10. See James Barr, *Biblical Words for Time* (Eugene, OR: Wipf & Stock, 1962) for a discussion of *kairos* and *chronos*. He is unconvinced that we can make philosophical or exegetical arguments about time exclusively from lexical evidence.

11. Charles Taylor, *A Secular Age* (Cambridge, MA: Harvard University Press, 2007), 59.

12. David Bentley Hart uses this phrase in his book *The Doors of the Sea* (Grand Rapids: Eerdmans, 2005).

13. Isaiah 40:6.

14. Luke 12:19.

15. Jeremiah 17:5, 7.

Habit 1 Begin

1. Alan Lakein, as quoted in Gregg, *Counterproductive*, 60.

2. "Estimated COVID-19 Burden," Centers for Disease Control and Prevention, updated November 16, 2021, https://www.cdc.gov/coronavirus/2019-ncov/cases-updates/burden.html.

3. Eula Biss, *On Immunity: An Inoculation* (Minneapolis: Graywolf, 2014), 29.

4. Robert Alter, *The Five Books of Moses: A Translation with Commentary* (New York: W. W. Norton, 2019), 11.

5. Alter uses the term "prose fiction," although this reveals his rejection of the historical truth of the Bible, which I don't share.

6. Robert Alter, *The Art of Biblical Narrative,* rev. and updated ed. (New York: Basic, 2011), 144.

7. Isaiah 40:26.

8. Isaiah 40:27.

9. 2 Samuel 18:33.

10. David Rooney, *About Time: A History of Civilization in Twelve Clocks* (New York: W. W. Norton, 2021), 203.

11. Biss, *On Immunity,* 5.

12. Wright, *Paul,* 45.

13. Wright, *Paul,* 45.

14. Fleming Rutledge, "Advent Begins in the Dark," in *Advent* (Grand Rapids: Eerdmans, 2018), Kindle ed.

15. Robert Alter, *The Hebrew Bible,* vol. 3 (New York: W. W. Norton, 2019), 466.

16. Alter, *Hebrew Bible,* 563.

17. Nicolas Watson and Jacqueline Jenkins, eds., *The Writings of Julian of Norwich* (University Park: Pennsylvania State University Press, 2006), 3.

18. Jeremiah 31:29.

19. Colossians 1:18.

20. Galatians 6:15.

21. 2 Corinthians 5:17.

22. Ephesians 2:4–5.

23. Colossians 3:10.

24. Romans 8:1.

25. 1 Chronicles 1:1–4 NLT.

26. Michael Wilcock, "1 and 2 Chronicles: Introduction," in *New Bible Commentary,* ed. by D. A. Carson et al. (Downers Grove, IL: IVP Academic, 1994), 388.

27. Wilcock, "1 and 2 Chronicles," 389.

28. Ezra 3:11–12.

29. Deuteronomy 32:18.

30. Stanley Hauerwas, *The Work of Theology* (Grand Rapids: Eerdmans, 2015), 90.

Habit 2 Receive

1. Miller, "Why You Should Start a Coronavirus Diary."

2. Timothy Fry, ed., *The Rule of Saint Benedict* (New York: Vintage Books, 1998), 30.

3. Fry, *Rule of Saint Benedict,* 4.

4. Fry, *Rule of Saint Benedict,* ix.

5. Kimberly Zapata, "How to Manifest Anything You Want or Desire," Oprah Daily, December 22, 2020, https://www.oprahdaily.com/life/a30244004/how-to-manifest-anything/.

6. "Zeptosecond—The Smallest Unit of Time Ever Measured," BBC, October 22, 2020, https://www.bbc.co.uk/newsround/54631056.

7. Alan Lightman, *Einstein's Dreams* (New York: Vintage, 1993), 21.

8. Dr. Amber Bowen, "The Tyranny of the Clock and the Gift of Time," lecture, Spring 2021 Honors Banquet, Anderson University. Shared by permission.

9. Bowen, "Tyranny of the Clock."

10. Jesmyn Ward, *Sing, Unburied, Sing: A Novel* (New York: Scribner, 2017), 233–34.

11. Dietrich Bonhoeffer, *Discipleship* (Minneapolis: Fortress, 2003), 221.

12. Here, I benefited from reading Carl Trueman's distillation of Charles Taylor's *Sources of the Self* in *The Rise and Triumph of the Modern Self* (Wheaton: Crossway, 2020), 39.

13. 1 Corinthians 4:7.

14. Amy Peterson, *Where Goodness Still Grows* (Nashville: W Publishing Group, 2020), 27.

15. Peterson, *Where Goodness Still Grows*, 27.

16. As quoted in Bethany Romano, "Racial Wealth Gap Continues to Grow between Black and White Families, Regardless of College Attainment," Brandeis University, July 16, 2018, heller.brandeis.edu/news/items/releases/2018/meschede-taylor-college-attainment-racial-wealth-gap.html.

17. W. H. Auden, "Horae Canonicae," in *Collected Poems* (New York: Vintage, 1991), 627.

18. John Milbank, *Being Reconciled* (London: Routledge, 2003), ix.

19. Acts 26:14.

20. Auden, "Horae Canonicae," 627.

Habit 3 Belong

1. Gregg, *Counterproductive*, 71–72.

2. Biss, *On Immunity*, 159–61.

3. Virginia Woolf, *A Room of One's Own* (New York: Harcourt, Brace and Company, 1982), 47.

4. Peter Wohlleben, *The Hidden Life of Trees* (Vancouver: Graystone Books, 2016), 169, 170.

5. Wohlleben, *Hidden Life of Trees*, 178.

6. Wohlleben, *Hidden Life of Trees*, 178.

7. Psalm 1:1–3.

8. Psalm 5:1; 17:1; 22:19.

9. Psalm 1:3 NJPS.

10. Adele Berlin and Marc Zvi Brettler, eds., *Tanakh: The Jewish Study Bible*, 2nd ed. (New York: Oxford University Press, 2014), 1,269.

11. Wohlleben, *Hidden Life of Trees*, 10.

12. Wohlleben, *Hidden Life of Trees*, 4.

13. 1 Corinthians 12:26.

14. Wohlleben, *Hidden Life of Trees*, 4.

15. Matthew 12:48.

16. Psalm 68:5–6.

17. Vanderkam, *I Know How She Does It*, 1.

18. James 1:27.

19. Kate Julian, "The Sex Recession," *Atlantic*, December 2018, https://www.theatlantic.com/magazine/archive/2018/12/the-sex-re cession/573949/.

20. Adam Grant, "There's a Name for the Blah You're Feeling: It's Called Languishing," *New York Times*, updated December 3, 2021, https://www.nytimes.com/2021/04/19/well/mind/covid-mental-health -languishing.html.

21. Rebecca Konyndyk DeYoung, *Glittering Vices* (Grand Rapids: Brazos, 2020), 104.

22. Jen Pollock Michel, "Letter from the Editor," *Imprint* 9 (2022): 3.

23. Katherine May, *Wintering* (New York: Riverhead Books, 2020), 69.

24. May, *Wintering*, 70–71.

25. Tish Harrison Warren, "How to Help Prepare Kids for Suffering," *New York Times*, October 10, 2021, https://www.nytimes.com/2021/10 /10/opinion/covid-trauma-kids.html.

26. Ecclesiastes 2:4–6, 9, 11.

27. Ecclesiastes 12:13.

28. Ecclesiastes 4:9–12.

29. Dietrich Bonhoeffer, *The Cost of Discipleship* (United Kingdom: SCM Press, 2015), 44.

30. Rebecca Konyndyk DeYoung, "Resistance to the Demands of Love," in *Christian Reflection: Acedia*, The Center for Christian Ethics, Baylor University, 2013, https://www.baylor.edu/content/services /document.php/212248.pdf.

Habit 4 Offer

1. 1 Corinthians 6:19–20.

2. Winn Collier, *A Burning in My Bones: The Authorized Biography of Eugene H. Peterson, Translator of The Message* (Colorado Springs: Waterbrook, 2021), xvi.

3. Jason Gay, "The Quiet Joys of the Very, Very Early Morning Club," *Wall Street Journal*, updated January 28, 2022, https://www.wsj.com

/articles/the-quiet-joys-of-the-very-very-very-early-club-11643398265
?st=wutaphclt6o7u00&reflink=article_email_share.

4. Andy Crouch discusses the meaning of this word in *The Life We're Looking For* (New York: Convergent, 2022), 125–26.

5. Isaiah 50:4–5.

6. Luke 1:38.

7. Robert Alter, *The Book of Psalms: A Translation with Commentary* (New York: W. W. Norton, 2007), 3.

8. Alter, *Book of Psalms*, 3.

9. Alter, *Book of Psalms*, 3.

10. Eugene Peterson, *Eat This Book: A Conversation in the Art of Reading* (Grand Rapids: Eerdmans, 2006), 2.

11. Peterson, *Eat This Book*, 3.

12. Crouch, *Life We're Looking For*, 126.

13. Crouch, *Life We're Looking For*, 129.

14. Swinton, *Becoming Friends of Time*, 117.

15. Marilyn McEntyre, *When Poets Pray* (Grand Rapids: Eerdmans, 2019), 25.

16. A. J. Swoboda, *Subversive Sabbath: The Surprising Power of Rest in a Nonstop World* (Grand Rapids: Brazos, 2018), 17.

17. John Cassian, "*Institutes* Book X. Of the Spirit of Accidie," Kevin Roddy's Webpage at UC Davis, accessed March 17, 2022, http://medieval.ucdavis.edu/120A/Cassian.html.

18. Cassian, "*Institutes* Book X."

19. Swinton, *Becoming Friends of Time*, 117.

20. Swinton, *Becoming Friends of Time*, 123.

21. Psalm 100:3.

22. These are examples of the call to prayer for each daily office found in *The Divine Hours*, edited by Phyllis Tickle. There are three volumes: *Prayers for Springtime*, *Prayers for Summertime*, and *Prayers for Autumn and Wintertime* (New York: Doubleday, 2000–2001).

23. Gregg, *Counterproductive*, 54.

24. Gregg, *Counterproductive*, 87.

25. Oliver Burkeman, "Why Time Management Is Ruining Our Lives," *The Guardian*, updated December 22, 2016, https://www.theguardian.com/technology/2016/dec/22/why-time-management-is-ruining-our-lives.

26. Laura Fabrycky, *Keys to Bonhoeffer's Haus: Exploring the World and Wisdom of Dietrich Bonhoeffer* (Minneapolis: Fortress, 2020), 98.

27. Fabrycky, *Keys to Bonhoeffer's Haus*, 99.

28. Fabrycky, *Keys to Bonhoeffer's Haus*, 117.

29. Fabrycky, *Keys to Bonhoeffer's Haus*, 120.

30. Laura Swan, *The Wisdom of the Beguines: The Forgotten Story of a Medieval Women's Movement* (Golden Bridges, NY: Bluebridge, 2014), 1.

31. Swan, *Wisdom of the Beguines*, 4.

32. Judith Oliver, "Devotional Psalters and the Study of Beguine Spirituality," *Vox Benedictina: A Journal of Translations from Monastic Sources* 9, no. 2 (1992): 199–225.

33. Psalm 109:1–2.

34. Psalm 137:1.

35. Wendell Berry, "1980: VI," in *A Timbered Choir* (Berkeley: Counterpoint, 1998), 30.

36. DeYoung, *Glittering Vices*, 62.

37. DeYoung, *Glittering Vices*, 58.

38. Berry, "1980: VI," 30.

Habit 5 Wait

1. Katrina Onstad, "The Miserable Truth about Online School," *Toronto Life*, February 18, 2021, https://torontolife.com/city/the-miserable -truth-about-online-school/.

2. Chase Peterson-Withorn, "How Much Money America's Billionaires Have Made during the Covid-19 Pandemic," *Forbes*, April 30, 2021, https://www.forbes.com/sites/chasewithorn/2021/04/30 /american-billionaires-have-gotten-12-trillion-richer-during-the-pan demic/?sh=bdbdd25f557e; Molly Kinder and Laura Stateler, "Amazon and Walmart Have Raked in Billions in Additional Profits during the Pandemic, and Shared Almost None of It with Their Workers," *Brookings*, December 22, 2020, https://www.brookings.edu/blog/the-avenue /2020/12/22/amazon-and-walmart-have-raked-in-billions-in-additional -profits-during-the-pandemic-and-shared-almost-none-of-it-with-their -workers/.

3. Jodi Kantor, Karen Weise, and Grace Ashford, "The Amazon That Customers Don't See," *New York Times*, June 5, 2021, https://www.ny times.com/interactive/2021/06/15/us/amazon-workers.html.

4. Psalm 13:1.

5. Mark 13:35.

6. Simone Weil, *Waiting on God* (New York: HarperCollins, 2009), 148.

7. Revelation 6:16.

8. Revelation 15:3 NLT.

9. Martin Luther King Jr., "Martin Luther King Jr.'s 'Letter from Birmingham Jail,'" *Atlantic*, accessed March 17, 2022, https://www.the atlantic.com/magazine/archive/2018/02/letter-from-a-birmingham-jail /552461/.

10. King, "Martin Luther King Jr.'s 'Letter from Birmingham Jail.'"

11. Luke 18:4–5.

12. Augustine, *Confessions* 9.22, trans. by Sarah Ruden (New York: Modern Library, 2017), 262.

13. James K. A. Smith, *On the Road with Saint Augustine: A Real-World Spirituality for Restless Hearts* (Grand Rapids: Brazos, 2019), 106.

14. Augustine, *Confessions* 3.21, trans. by Henry Chadwick (Oxford: Oxford University Press, 1991), 50, 51.

15. Smith, *On the Road with Saint Augustine*, 113.

16. Exodus 14:13–14.

17. Isaiah 30:18 VOICE.

18. Rutledge, "Advent Begins in the Dark."

19. See John 15:7.

20. Ecclesiastes 1:15.

21. Jeffrey Meyers, as quoted in David Gibson, *Living Life Backward: How Ecclesiastes Teaches Us to Live in Light of the End* (Wheaton: Crossway, 2017), chap. 2, Kindle ed.

22. Psalm 127:1.

Habit 6 Practice

1. As quoted in Kathleen Norris, *Acedia & Me* (New York: Riverhead, 2008), 152.

2. I've benefited enormously from this definition of acedia by Rebecca DeYoung in her essay "Resistance to the Demands of Love."

3. DeYoung, *Glittering Vices*, 108.

4. N. T. Wright, *After You Believe: Why Christian Character Matters* (New York: HarperCollins, 2010), chap. 1, Kindle ed.

5. Brother Lawrence, *The Practice of the Presence of God* (Boston: Shambhala, 2005), 23.

6. Brother Lawrence, *Practice of the Presence of God*, ix.

7. Acts 17:28.

8. In *Counterproductive*, Melissa Gregg has dedicated the second section of the book to the subject of practice and the "athleticism" implied in a lot of time management advice.

9. Matthew Crawford, *The World beyond Your Head: On Becoming an Individual in an Age of Distraction* (New York: Allen Lane, 2015), 13.

10. Kathleen Norris, *Amazing Grace: A Vocabulary of Faith* (New York: Riverhead Books, 1998), 17.

11. Brother Lawrence, *Practice of the Presence of God*, 5.

12. Brother Lawrence, *Practice of the Presence of God*, VIII.

13. Margaret Guenther, *At Home in the World: A Rule of Life for the Rest of Us* (New York: Church Publishing, 2006), chap. 1, Kindle ed.

14. Swoboda, *Subversive Sabbath*, 45.

15. Fry, *Rule of Saint Benedict*, 20.

16. Fry, *Rule of Saint Benedict*, 42.

17. Swinton, *Becoming Friends of Time*, 26.

18. Weil, *Waiting on God*, 29.

19. Weil, *Waiting on God*, 72.

20. Brother Lawrence, *Practice of the Presence of God*, 9.

21. Alan Kreider, *The Patient Ferment of the Early Church: The Improbable Rise of Christianity in the Roman Empire* (Grand Rapids: Baker Academic, 2016), 140.

22. Kreider, *Patient Ferment*, 141.

23. Phyllis Tickle, ed., *The Divine Hours: Prayers for Autumn and Wintertime* (New York: Doubleday, 2000).

24. Philippians 4:9.

25. Psalm 1:1–2.

26. Derek Kidner, "Proverbs 31," in *The Wisdom of Proverbs, Job, and Ecclesiastes*.

27. Derek Kidner, "Wisdom," in *Proverbs*.

28. Kidner, "Wisdom," in *Proverbs*.

29. I read this in a review copy of Mark Sayers, *Reappearing Church: The Hope for Renewal in the Rise of Our Post-Christian Culture* (Chicago: Moody, 2019).

30. DeYoung, *Glittering Vices*, 101.

31. C. S. Lewis, *The Screwtape Letters* (New York: HarperCollins, 1996), 12.

Habit 7 Enjoy

1. You can subscribe to Heather Moffitt's *The Incurable* at https://theincurable.substack.com.

2. Heather Moffitt, "The Paradox of Pain," *The Incurable* (blog), May 14, 2021, https://theincurable.substack.com/p/the-paradox-of-pain?s=r.

3. Heather Moffitt, "Six Months Later, I'm Still Here," *The Incurable* (blog), November 7, 2021, https://theincurable.substack.com/p/six-months-later-im-still-here?s=r.

4. See Psalm 126:6–7.

5. Psalm 90:15, 10.

6. Psalm 90:14.

7. Readers of Annie Dillard will recognize I've borrowed this image from *Pilgrim at Tinker Creek*.

8. Philippians 4:4.

9. *OED Online*, s.v. "enjoy," Oxford University Press, accessed April 15, 2022, www.oed.com/view/Entry/62406.

10. Andrew Warrick, "'Jingle Jangle' Makes Christmas Exhausting," *The Michigan Daily*, November 15, 2020, https://www.michigandaily.com/arts/film/jingle-jangle-makes-christmas-exhausting/.

11. Psalm 34:11–13.

12. Psalm 19:1.

13. Psalm 84:10.

14. Jeremiah 31:12–13.

15. Marilynne Robinson, *Gilead* (New York: Farrar, Straus & Giroux, 2004), 245.

16. Robinson, *Gilead*, 243.

17. Luke 1:44.

18. As quoted in Crawford, *World beyond Your Head*, 100.

19. C. S. Lewis, *Surprised by Joy: The Shape of My Early Life* (repr., New York: HarperOne, 2017), 209.

20. As quoted in Crawford, *World beyond Your Head*, 96.

21. Crawford, *World beyond Your Head*, 25.

22. David Allen, *Getting Things Done: The Art of Stress-Free Productivity* (New York: Penguin, 2015), chap. 4, Kindle ed.

23. Full Focus, "The Full Focus Planner," accessed March 22, 2022, https://fullfocus.co/planner/.

24. Christina Crook, *Good Burdens: How to Live Joyfully in the Digital Age* (Halifax: Nimbus, 2021), 9.

25. Crook, *Good Burdens*, 9

26. Hartmut Rosa, *Social Acceleration: A New Theory of Modernity* (New York: Columbia University Press, 2015).

27. Andrew Root, *The Congregation in a Secular Age* (Grand Rapids: Baker Academic, 2021), 216.

28. Root, *Congregation in a Secular Age*, 216.

29. *OED Online*, s.v. "enjoy."

30. "Gratitude," *The Monk Manual*, accessed February 9, 2022, https://monkmanual.com/pages/gratitude.

31. Jim Manney, *What Do You Really Want?: St. Ignatius Loyola and the Art of Discernment* (Huntington, IN: Our Sunday Visitor, 2015), chap. 3, Kindle ed.

Habit 8 Remember

1. Fry, *Rule of Saint Benedict*, 12.

2. Fry, *Rule of Saint Benedict*, 13, emphasis added.

3. Robert Frost, "The Road Not Taken," in *The Poetry of Robert Frost*, ed. by Edward Connery Lathem (New York: St. Martin's Griffin, 1969), 105.

4. Frost, "The Road Not Taken."

5. Hebrews 11:7–8, 31.

6. Daniel 5:23.

7. Burkeman, *Four Thousand Weeks*, 12–13.

8. Craig Bartholomew, *Ecclesiastes*, Baker Commentary on the Old Testament Wisdom and Psalms series, ed. by Tremper Longman III (Grand Rapids: Baker Academic, 2009), 166.

9. R. E. Murphy, *Ecclesiastes*, Word Biblical Commentary series, vol. 23 (Dallas: Word, 1992), 39.

10. Bartholomew, *Ecclesiastes*, 162.

11. See Ecclesiastes 3:1–8.

12. Bartholomew, *Ecclesiastes*, 171.

13. According to information provided to me by the museum's curators, this statue, called "Christ of the Holy Sepulchre," was sculpted by an unnamed Upper-Rhenish or Western Swiss artist and acquired by Prince Johann II von Liechtenstein in 1909.

14. Alexandra Hanzl, email to the author, June 28, 2021. Used by permission.

15. Isaiah 40:1.

16. Douglas Kaine McKelvey, *Every Moment Holy*, vol. 2 (Nashville: Rabbit Room Press, 2021), xiv.

17. As quoted in Michelle Duster, *Ida B. the Queen: The Extraordinary Life and Legacy of Ida B. Wells* (New York: One Signal Publishers, 2021), 48–49.

18. Allen, *Getting Things Done*, chap. 11, Kindle ed.

19. Sarah Goodhue, *The Copy of a Valedictory and Monitory Writing* (repr., Boston: Metcalf and Co., 1850), 3, https://archive.org/details/copy ofvaledictor00good/page/n3/mode/2up.

20. Goodhue, *Copy of a Valedictory and Monitory Writing*, 6.

21. Augustine, *Confessions*, 11.32 (1991), 239.

22. Augustine, *Confessions*, 11.6 (1991), 224.

23. Augustine, *Confessions*, 11.40 (1991), 244.

24. Augustine, *Confessions*, 11.41 (1991), 245.

25. Watson and Jenkins, eds., *Writings of Julian of Norwich*, 139.

26. Isaiah 11:1.

Afterword

1. Bonnie Blackburn and Leofranc Holford-Stevens, *The Oxford Companion to the Year* (Oxford: Oxford University Press, 2013), 204–5.

2. Blackburn and Holford-Stevens, *Oxford Companion to the Year*, vi.

3. Blackburn and Holford-Stevens, *Oxford Companion to the Year*, 689.

4. Blackburn and Holford-Stevens, *Oxford Companion to the Year*, 688–89.

5. Rooney, *About Time*, 5.

6. I owe my understanding of these first-century dynamics to N. T. Wright and his book *Paul: A Biography* (San Francisco: HarperOne, 2018).

7. Genesis 42:21.

8. Alter, *Five Books of Moses*, 242.

9. Fry, *Rule of Saint Benedict*, 13.

10. Davis, *Getting Involved with God*, 92.

Jen Pollock Michel is the award-winning author of *Teach Us to Want, Keeping Place, Surprised by Paradox,* and *A Habit Called Faith.* She holds a BA in French from Wheaton College and an MA in Literature from Northwestern University, and she is also a student in Seattle Pacific's MFA program. Jen is a wife and mother of five and hosts the *Englewood Review of Books* podcast.

The Leading Outlet
for Book News, Reviews, and
Conversations for Christian Readers

The *Englewood Review of Books* podcast is an ongoing, thoughtful conversation about the reading life brought to you by the editors and contributors to the *Englewood Review of Books*. Hosted by Jen Pollock Michel, and joined by a rotating cast of ERB contributors, panelists discuss how they engage in reading, what it means to read well, and of course the books and writers they enjoy. Expect lively discussions about books from all genres, from a rotating group of writers and readers who care about reading well.

AVAILABLE WHEREVER PODCASTS ARE FOUND

@erbooks @ERBks

www.EnglewoodReview.org

A Bible Reading Experience for Both the Convinced and the Curious

With vulnerable storytelling and insightful readings of both Old and New Testament passages, Jen Pollock Michel invites you into a forty-day Bible reading experience. Vividly translating ancient truths for a secular age, Michel highlights how the biblical text invites us to see, know, live, love, and obey. The daily reflection questions and weekly discussion guides invite both believers and doubters alike to explore how faith might grow into a life-defining habit.

Connect with Jen

Head to **jenpollockmichel.com** to sign up for her Monday letters, to learn about her speaking, or to send her a message.

And follow her on social media!

   jenpmichel